EFFECTIVE TEACHING

PRINCIPLES AND PRACTICE

EFFECTIVE TEACHING

PRINCIPLES AND PRACTICE

Marilyn Kourilsky
University of California, Los Angeles

Lory Quaranta
University of California, Los Angeles

Scott, Foresman and Company
Glenview, Illinois   London, England

This book is dedicated to our wonderful children:
Shari Kourilsky
&
Luke and Seth Quaranta

Library of Congress Cataloging-in-Publication Data

Kourilsky, Marilyn L.
  Effective teaching.

  Bibliography: p.
  Includes index.
  1. Teaching. 2. Curriculum planning—United States.
3. Public schools—United States. I. Quaranta, Lory.
II. Title.
LB1025.2.K669 1987   371.1′02   86-20347
ISBN 0-673-18386-6

PREFACE

Teaching is a challenging, complex, and rewarding profession. There is an art to effective teaching that can be acquired and refined. It is, in part, through the thorough acquisition of pedagogical skills and the sensitivity to individual learning requirements that one becomes a gifted teacher. In having a repertoire of instructional strategies available, one can generate the most appropriate and meaningful learning environment for one's students. Through a clear understanding of curricular principles, one can match objectives and materials to individual learners.

Effective Teaching: Principles and Practice is for teachers—those in training and those already in the classroom. It covers the underlying skills necessary for curriculum development, focusing on initiating, developing, implementing, and evaluating written lesson and unit plans. In addition, the book presents a wide range of instructional strategies, from the lecture method to experience-based instruction, with an emphasis on translating each strategy into classroom practice. Learning principles and classroom discipline techniques are also explored because they play a pivotal role in the creation of a successful classroom.

The diagram, "Key Elements of Curriculum Development and the Instructional Process," reflects a major focus of this book, the development of curriculum and the instructional process. The learner is always at the center of this process and is the reason for the extreme care taken in following the sequence.

In addition to being curriculum planners, teachers are also instructional decision-makers. In this book, three major types of instructional decisions are highlighted. First, teacher-led instruction is an approach whereby the teacher initiates, directs, and monitors the instructional sequence. A primary example of this strategy is the lecture method. In Chapter Two the lecture method will be discussed as a form of communication. A second approach is student-centered instruction, wherein students are often the initiators and always the primary vehicles of the learning experience and interaction. Examples of student-centered instruction are experience-based instruction (Chapter Five), role-playing (Chapter Five), and inquiry-based instruction (Chapter Six). Technology offers a third type of instructional approach available to teachers. Audiovisual resources and computers, discussed in Chapter Eight, are examples of technological components that affect instruction. In this approach, the content has already been generated by the technological vehicle itself. The decisions of the teachers are whether, when, and how to use the available resources.

This book has been written with elementary and secondary teachers in mind; examples applying to both are provided as often as possible. For training teachers, we advocate substantial observation and participation in the classroom before student teaching. (We have been involved in implementing a model based on observation and participation at the UCLA Teacher Education Laboratory.) Teachers in training are encouraged to apply as many of the concepts and principles of this book as possible in their observation of the classroom or participation in it. This application will broaden their understanding of the concepts and principles and make them more useful for later, direct teaching experiences.

For teachers in training and for staff development purposes, we have provided a set of practice activities in Appendix A. These activities are based on the key instructional concepts and classroom applications presented in the text. Appendix B provides a set of worksheets and blank forms that may be pulled out of the book and used in assessing, planning, and executing instruction.

The need for excellent, well-trained, and highly motivated teachers cannot be disputed. Teachers *can* make a positive difference in the daily and future lives of students. Our responsibility as professionals in education is to become the best qualified and most well-rounded teachers we can be.

Acknowledgments

We would like to thank Jim Popham, who has made significant contributions to the field of education, especially in the areas of evaluation and instructional decision making, for sharing his insights and materials in the writing of this book. His personal and professional generosity and standards of excellence are much appreciated. Special thanks are due to Susie Sugerman, Dina Passi, and Julie Branica for graciously allowing their excellent unit and lesson plans to be subjected to an intense public critique. Of course, their plans were used because the critique revealed so many of the merits we wanted to demonstrate of such plans.

In appreciation for their contribution to this book, we further recognize Elizabeth Barry for stimulating the work on learning centers and Shari Kourilsky for critiquing the unit and lesson plans. We would also like to thank Ashley Parker for her dedicated editorial assistance in preparing this text and Jim Laney for his comments and observations.

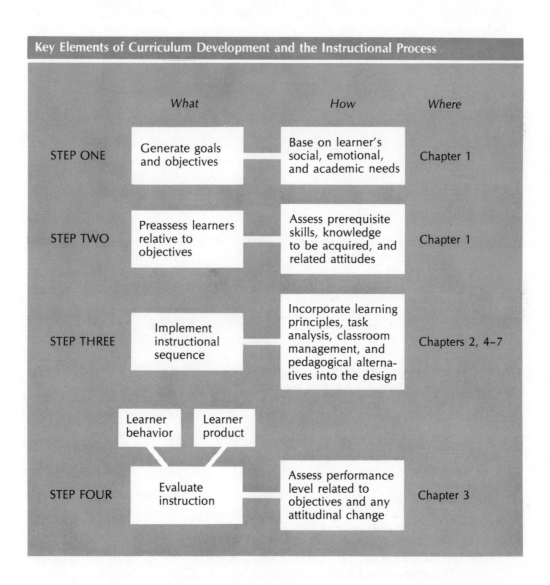

Key Elements of Curriculum Development and the Instructional Process

	What	*How*	*Where*
STEP ONE	Generate goals and objectives	Base on learner's social, emotional, and academic needs	Chapter 1
STEP TWO	Preassess learners relative to objectives	Assess prerequisite skills, knowledge to be acquired, and related attitudes	Chapter 1
STEP THREE	Implement instructional sequence	Incorporate learning principles, task analysis, classroom management, and pedagogical alternatives into the design	Chapters 2, 4–7
STEP FOUR	Learner behavior / Learner product / Evaluate instruction	Assess performance level related to objectives and any attitudinal change	Chapter 3

CONTENTS

EFFECTIVE TEACHING

PRINCIPLES AND PRACTICE

PART ONE

CURRICULUM, TEACHING, AND EVALUATION: PRINCIPLES AND INTERRELATIONS

CHAPTER ONE

CURRICULUM DEVELOPMENT

The first major step in the strategic planning of teaching is deciding *what to teach*. This involves the specification of instructional goals and objectives and the concomitant preassessment of the learners to determine where they stand in relation to these goals and objectives.

GOAL STATEMENTS AND OBJECTIVES

In generating goals and objectives for learners, the key is to determine what the students need to achieve, develop, and understand or appreciate. In some school districts, courses of study for each grade level have been developed, providing teachers with a framework of desired educational outcomes; other sources include elementary basal programs, curriculum guides, and secondary subject area textbooks. Of course, teachers are the primary source of goals and objectives for their particular learners and must be skillful at writing and selecting appropriate educational goals and measurable instructional objectives.

    Goals are broad statements of desired educational outcomes. They point to the target goals of instruction and provide the pillars on which the subsequent learning experiences are built. Examples of goal statements are:

The learner will develop
- basic math skills
- an appreciation of poetry
- an awareness of body parts
- an understanding of the Civil War

As you can see, these statements are useful in designating the overall goals of the instructional program but lack the specificity essential in the actual implementation of an instructional sequence. For such purposes, clear and measurable objectives are needed.

To generate an instructional *objective,* one must take a goal statement and determine the specific student behavior(s) which would serve to further this goal. This specified behavior must be readily observable by the teacher. For example, a learner may be observed exhibiting the following behaviors: (1) reading orally, (2) raising his/her hand, (3) bouncing a ball, or (4) writing an essay. On the other hand, one could not *directly* observe a student understanding verbs or knowing woodworking safety rules. To operationalize the objectives, any behavior must be defined in ways that allow the teacher to observe and determine the learner's progress relative to the stated objective.

An instructional objective should meet the following criteria:

1. It sets the situation or condition for learning.
   Examples: On an essay test, . . .
   In a role-playing situation, . . .
   After viewing a film on endangered species, . . .
   When working in small groups, . . .
2. It defines the learner's behavior in measurable and observable terms.
   Examples: Given a math worksheet, the student will *circle* the correct answer for each of the ten addition problems.
   On a map of our solar system, the student will correctly *label* the planets and *color* them in.
3. It states the minimal level of performance required.
   Examples: On an outline map of Europe, the student will color in and label *at least three* major mountain ranges.
   In an essay, the student will include *two* supporting details for each topic sentence.

Now, putting it all together, the following social studies objectives provide examples of the essential components of complete instructional objectives as just described:

- On an outline map of the United States, the student will correctly label at least three pioneer routes to the Far West. (1) The condition = *on an outline map* of the United States; (2) the measurable, observable term = *label;* and (3) the level of performance = *at least three routes.*
- In a problem-solving discussion, the student will orally state at least two reasons why bananas are kept at cool temperatures before they are sent out to markets. (1) The condition = *in a problem-solving discussion;* (2) the measurable, observable term = *orally state;* and (3) the level of performance = *two reasons.*

- On a written examination, the student will list four major differences between cities in India and cities in Japan. (1) the condition = *on a written examination;* (2) the measurable, observable term = *list;* and (3) the level of performance = *four major differences.*
- After viewing a film on the Civil War, the student will write a paragraph summary containing three major facts about the war derived from watching the film. (1) The condition = *after viewing a film;* (2) the measurable, observable term = *write;* and (3) the level of performance = *three major facts.*
- After listening to a guest speaker, the student will draw a picture of the career presented, depicting one task/service representative of the career. (1) The condition = *after listening to a guest speaker;* (2) the measurable, observable term = *draw;* and (3) the level of performance = *one task/service.*

Example at the Primary Level. Given a set of wooden blocks, small groups of students will construct a miniature city, with at least five buildings. (1) The condition = *given a set of wooden blocks;* (2) the measurable, observable term = *construct;* and (3) the level of performance = *a city with five buildings.*

The verbs categorized in Table 1–1 may be useful in generating instructional objectives; they are arranged by specific curriculum areas. Some verbs may be used in more than one area.

It is useful to be aware of existing categories of educational objectives, often referred to as taxonomies of objectives. The following taxonomies provide a context within which to classify and conceptualize student learning and development: (1) the cognitive domain, (2) the affective domain, and (3) the psychomotor domain.

The majority of the objectives generated for and applied to learners are cognitive objectives, which involve intellectual processes. Benjamin Bloom has developed a widely used hierarchy of levels of intellectual behavior, often called Bloom's Taxonomy, which classifies mental processes in the cognitive domain (Bloom, 1956). The six levels of this hierarchy are (1) *knowledge* — remembering, (2) *comprehension* — grasping the meaning and intent of material, (3) *application* — bringing appropriate generalizations to bear in new situations, (4) *analysis* — breakdown of material into constituent parts and detection of the relationships among the parts and of the way they are organized, (5) *synthesis* — putting together elements and parts to form a whole, and, finally, (6) *evaluation* — making judgments in relation to specific criteria (e.g., values).

This hierarchy is helpful in delineating increasing levels of complexity in intellectual processes. It is vital to incorporate this range of levels into students' learning experiences to promote intellectual development and stimulation. Applying this conceptual hierarchy to objective writing, the following list provides sample verbs which correspond to each level represented:

Table 1–1 VERBS USED IN INSTRUCTIONAL OBJECTIVES WITHIN CURRICULUM AREA

Foreign Language	*Language Arts*	*Mathematics*
accent	abbreviate	bisect
pronounce	alphabetize	compute
read	capitalize	estimate
recite	indent	graph
state	punctuate	measure
translate	summarize	solve

Music	*Physical Education and Health Safety*	*Reading*
clap	bat	analyze
harmonize	carry	describe
hum	fasten	infer
play	grasp	order
sing	hop	reconstruct
strum	march	select
	stretch	
	taste	
	tie	
	uncover	
	wash	
	wear	

Religion	*Science*	*Social Studies*
accept	demonstrate	cite
describe	dissect	compile
interpret	feed	evaluate
order	plant	map
respond	report	quote
select	weigh	support

1. *Knowledge level:* recall, label, memorize
2. *Comprehension level:* locate, describe, restate
3. *Application level:* operate, interpret, demonstrate
4. *Analysis level:* compare, analyze, test
5. *Synthesis level:* design, organize, formulate
6. *Evaluation level:* predict, assess, judge

Taking the application of this hierarchical structure one step further, a classroom example, "The Albatross," is provided illustrating questions and activities which represent each of the six levels.

Topic: The Albatross

Seventh-Grade Science Wildlife Unit

1. *Knowledge level:* List three physical characteristics of the albatross.
2. *Comprehension level:* Describe the feeding habits of the albatross.
3. *Application level:* Give the reason behind these nicknames which sailors gave to the albatross: "Stupid gull" and "Gooney."
4. *Analysis level:* Compare three species of the albatross in terms of their distinguishing physical characteristics.
5. *Synthesis level:* Design a collage representing the natural habitat and physical characteristics of the albatross.
6. *Evaluation:* Predict what would happen if carnivores were to enter the natural habitat of the albatross.

This taxonomy is not the sole one in existence or use, but it is representative of the ones available. Recently, some teachers have been using a revised and somewhat condensed version of Bloom's six-tiered hierarchy. It keeps levels one and two intact but combines levels three through six, as described here:

Level One: Memorizing the concept. Student can recall and provide information which has been presented; information is in the same basic form as when presented. *Example:* Student can orally recite the names of the four seasons after the lesson.

Level Two: Applying the concept when asked. Student can demonstrate a working knowledge and basic understanding of the given concept/fact/skill by providing in a new format the information which has been presented. *Example:* After a series of grammar lectures, the student can write an essay using correct punctuation.

Level Three: Generating the concept in a new context. Given a problem situation (with the concept not labeled or specifically called for), student can appropriately demonstrate internalization of the concept. *Example:* In a simulation activity following a unit of study on the U.S. government, the student role-plays the executive functions of the U.S. president.

Experiences in school and personal learning are not limited to the cognitive domain. In the affective domain are attitudes, feelings, emotions, and moral characteristics, important aspects of student development. A hierarchy has also been developed for this domain (Krathwohl, Bloom, & Masia). The levels are explicated here:

1. *Receiving:* a state of awareness; a willingness to receive; selected attention. *Example:* Students demonstrate a willingness to listen to a recording of Australian folk music, but express no strong feeling for it one way or the other.

2. *Responding:* an open attitude toward responding; a willingness to respond; a satisfaction derived from responding. *Example:* Students decide to respond to the presented music by clapping along and experience pleasure/satisfaction from participating.
3. *Valuing:* An acceptance of values; a preference for a value; making a commitment related to the value. *Example:* Students accept the value of folk music, relate it to their own value system, and form a commitment related to the importance of music.
4. *Organization:* a conceptualization of a value; an organization of a value system. *Example:* Students incorporate their new appreciation for folk music into their existing value system for music and perhaps other areas (cultures, poetry, etc.).
5. *Characterization by a value complex:* a formation of a generalized set; a manifestation of the value complex. *Example:* Students incorporate the value of music into their personal lives and apply the concept to their personal hobbies, interests, careers, etc.

The levels of this hierarchy may appear less readily distinguishable from one another and less clearly observable in students than those in the cognitive domain. However, through the observation of students, the administration of attitude questionnaires, and class discussions, such growth and attitudinal change can be interpreted.

When developing curriculum, it is essential to consider and incorporate affective objectives whenever possible and appropriate. Such goals as a healthy self-concept, an expressed willingness to participate in a learning experience, and a personal value system are indeed worthy goals, reflected in the application of the affective domain.

The third category of educational objectives is the psychomotor domain, which refers to bodily movements and bodily control. Such physical abilities may be movement patterns or a specific physical skill or skill sequence. The main types of behaviors represented in the psychomotor domain are as follows (Singer & Dick, 1974): (1) contacting, manipulating, and/or moving an object; (2) controlling the body or objects, as in balancing; (3) moving and/or controlling the body or parts of the body in space in a brief timed act or sequence under predictable and/or unpredictable conditions; and (4) making controlled, appropriate sequential movements (not time restricted) in a predictable and/or unpredictable and changing situation.

A hierarchical structure of psychomotor objectives, developed by Elizabeth Simpson (1966–67) is outlined here:

1. *Perception.* Using the five sense organs to gain an awareness of objectives and to translate this perception to action. *Example:* When playing volleyball, the student uses sight, hearing, and tactile stimulation to become aware of the physical

elements of the game. (Taste and smell apply to many physical activities.) The combination of these sensory perceptions is displayed in a kinesthetic (bodily) response.

2. *Set.* Being ready to mentally, physically, and emotionally respond. *Example:* A student in a diving position, ready to swim laps in the pool, demonstrates physical preparation and an attitudinal readiness for the activity.

3. *Guided response.* Assistance is provided to the learner through an overt behavioral act, such as role-modeling the desired behavior or through individual trial and error. *Example:* After a teacher-led demonstration of playing scales on the piano, the student practices the scales independently.

4. *Mechanism.* The learned physical response has become habitual. *Example:* During a woodworking session, the student exhibits adherence to safety rules and demonstrates basic woodworking skills.

5. *Complex overt response.* A complex motor act is demonstrated with skill and efficiency. *Example:* During a typing session, the student completes the given assignment with no errors and a high level of speed.

6. *Adaption.* Altering responses in new situations. *Example:* After having learned to play basketball, the student applies learned skills to play water basketball for the first time.

7. *Origination.* Creating new acts. *Example:* After completing a course in diving, the student creates new dives, combining learned skills and physical experimentation.

Psychomotor skills constitute an important part of a person's development. Throughout the elementary and secondary school years such objectives should be carefully planned and implemented as part of the student's total curriculum. Such activities as typing and playing a musical instrument, in addition to physically-based games and sports, serve to promote mental alertness and activity and physical health.

The lists of verbs in Table 1–2 may be useful in generating instructional objectives according to the three taxonomies discussed. These lists are by no means exhaustive but are provided to illustrate verbs which reflect observable pupil behaviors within the three domains.

PREASSESSMENT

In conjunction with developing appropriate and thorough goals and objectives for learners, the teacher must formulate a *preassessment* strategy to determine student performance levels before instruction related to the given objectives. There are three major areas to consider in the preassessment of

Table 1-2. VERBS USED IN INSTRUCTIONAL OBJECTIVES WITHIN DOMAIN

Cognitive Domain	Affective Domain	Psychomotor Domain
compare	accept	assemble
define	aid	carve
distinguish	contribute	construct
identify	greet	drill
list	interact	mix
match	participate	pat
paraphrase	praise	saw
point	react	sketch
regroup	volunteer	stamp
reunite		
select		

learners: (1) the prerequisite skills and knowledge related to the target objectives; (2) the specific skills and knowledge put forth in the target objectives; and (3) the attitude (emotional response) of the learners toward the content covered in the target objectives.

First, when writing an objective for a particular group of learners, the teacher must consider what prerequisite skills are needed for students to attend to and potentially master the given objectives. Often preliminary instruction or review may be necessary before initiating an instructional sequence.

Second, learners must be assessed in terms of the desired performance level set forth in the objective. If students have already mastered a given objective, then valuable instructional time would be lost if they were to participate in the planned instructional sequence; additionally, the motivation and interest level of these students could be seriously diminished.

The third key area in preassessment is the assessment of students' attitudes and interest levels related to the designated objectives. This factor is important because it may influence the likelihood of instructional success. Negative attitudes need to be addressed and somewhat altered to strengthen student achievement. Positive attitudes need to be noted and then nurtured.

For example, let us say that a teacher has formulated the following goals and objective for learners:

- Goals: The student will develop writing skills. The student will develop a positive attitude toward grammar.
- Objective: At the end of the lesson, the student will be able to underline the verb and circle the subject of eight out of ten given sentences on a worksheet.

The teacher should assess the learners' knowledge and attitudes before instruction to determine what they understand about subjects and verbs.

Some students may fully understand them and simply need to review them briefly. Others may be unfamiliar with the concept of parts of speech or specific functions of nouns and verbs within sentences. Additionally, students' attitudes toward grammar may hinder or enhance their performance. For the instruction to truly meet the needs of the students and extend their knowledge, the teacher must, before implementing instruction, carefully assess what students know and need to know.

Turning now from the *why* of preassessment to the *how to* there are two basic approaches to administering preassessment: formal and informal preassessment. Formal preassessment refers to specific information gathered systematically. A number of approaches may be taken, such as analysis of previous test scores or specific results of criterion-referenced instruments (see Chapter 3), one-on-one interviews with students, review of a student's cumulative records, or administration of a questionnaire. Data collected through such means are typically used to provide the teacher with an attitudinal and skills-based profile of individual learners; compiled data may also yield helpful comparative profiles of groups of learners.

As the name implies, informal preassessment is typically conducted more informally and usually provides a more generalized view of learners' abilities and attitudes. Usually done through observation of student behavior or oral discussions, informal preassessment yields less specific data regarding learners' skills but may be very useful in providing a holistic view of student performance and an attitudinal profile of a group of learners. An example of such preassessment would be a teacher who has presented a lesson on mammals and seeks an on-the-spot assessment of student progress before presenting new content. The teacher may ask the class to signal somehow as a question is asked to determine if an adequate mastery of key concepts has been achieved. The teacher may ask students to point up for yes and point down for no as questions about content are asked.

Generating goals and objectives and implementing preassessment techniques constitute a major part of the instructional process. If these elements are carefully executed, the learners stand a very good chance of encountering an instructional program whose planning is viable and highly appropriate.

TASK ANALYSIS

After generating complete instructional objectives and confirming through preassessment students' readiness to perform the objectives, the next step is to develop a *task analysis*. Essentially, task analysis involves the breaking down of complex learning or learning tasks into simpler components (steps) and then sequencing those parts to ensure a more cohesive and effective instructional sequence.

Figure 1-1. SAMPLE TASK ANALYSIS

Target Behavior
Working in small groups, the students go through the inventing process to create a new and original invention.

En Route Behavior
Students learn about patents, models, and prototypes through lecture, filmstrip, and reading.

En Route Behavior
Students read about one chosen inventor and his/her invention. Write one page report. Give two minute oral presentation.

En Route Behavior
Students watch film on famous inventors and their inventions; discuss; write one paragraph summary.

Entry-level Behaviors
Students understand the term "inventor." Students can write and read at the sixth grade level. Students can express ideas orally.

Initially the teacher must decide on the target learner behavior to be demonstrated at the end of the instructional sequence; this is reflected in the *terminal,* or long-range objective. Sample terminal objectives are provided here:

1. By the end of the telling-time unit, the student will be able to state orally the time by the half-hour when given a clock with manipulatable hands, set at specific times by the teacher.

2. By the end of the geography lessons, the student will be able to label correctly three major rivers, one major mountain range, five major cities, and two main products of South America on an outline map.

To master these terminal objectives, students need to perform intermediate or en route behaviors. The teacher actually establishes the terminal objectives and then traces back through the required sequential steps necessary to arrive at the objective. The baseline, or entry-level, behaviors of the learner are the prerequisite skills and knowledge base the student must possess to embark on the task-analyzed instructional sequence.

A sample task analysis, using the theme of inventors (Caney, 1985), is presented in Figure 1–1.

As the reader can see from Figure 1–1, the learner behaviors listed are not stated as operationalized instructional objectives. Preliminary task analysis is actually a curriculum planning device which would in turn lead to the generation of a corresponding set of instructional objectives from which to design and finally implement the instructional sequence. (See Chapter 2 for lesson and unit planning.)

Task analysis may be done for such instructional sequences as a unit of study, a series of lectures or demonstrations, or even a single lesson plan. The key is to establish a firm grasp and complete view of the given instructional sequence, yielding the required baseline behavior and any necessary instructional and conceptual steps which will need to be taken for learners to achieve mastery of the terminal objective.

CHAPTER SUMMARY

In this chapter, the essential components of curriculum design have been presented: the generation of complete instructional objectives, the rationale for the application of educational taxonomies, the use of preassessment strategies, and the process of task analyzing instruction. Through the effective use of these complementary instructional skills in the development of curriculum, the instructor provides the foundation for appropriate and well-planned instruction.

References

Bloom, B. S., Krathwohl, D. R., et al. *Taxonomy of educational objectives: Handbook I, Cognitive domain.* New York: Longmans, Green, 1956.

Caney, S. *Steven Caney's Invention Book.* New York: Workman Publishing, 1985.

Krathwohl, D. R., Bloom, B. S., & Masia, B. *Taxonomy of educational objectives: Handbook II, Affective domain.* New York: David McKay Co., 1964.

Simpson, E. *The classification of educational objectives, psychomotor domain. Illinois Teacher of Home Economics, 10* (Winter): 110–144, 1966–1967.

Singer, R., & Dick, W. *Teaching physical education: A systems approach.* Boston: Houghton Mifflin Co., 1964.

CHAPTER TWO

LEARNING AND TEACHING

Once the instructional goals and objectives have been formulated, a preassessment strategy developed, and a task analysis designed (see Chapter One), the teacher must then decide how to actually achieve the desired educational outcomes. Crucial in this process are (1) understanding and applying key learning principles, (2) using strategic planning to design well-structured written plans (lesson and unit plans), and (3) selecting and implementing effective strategies and classroom management techniques.

LEARNING PRINCIPLES

Learning principles are theoretical constructs which yield important implications for successful achievement in the classroom. Through research and field application, these principles have become useful tools in maximizing teacher time, instructional resources, and student potential. Numerous principles of learning are found in the literature and a variety of terms applied to them. We have selected eight key learning principles which we feel make the most significant contribution to the practitioner — the teacher in the classroom trying to create an optimal learning environment.

The learning principles presented here will first be defined and then translated into classroom practice through a variety of grade-level examples:

Task Description

Research indicates that students perform better and achieve more in learning situations when they are told early in the instructional sequence what they are intended to learn or acquire, that is, given a *task description*. Teachers generally go through careful and deliberate planning to generate goals and objectives; it is very helpful to learners if this information is shared with them. Sharing it establishes a clear understanding of the task/activity in which learners will be engaged and creates a feeling of shared ownership in the desired mastery of the target objectives. As adults, we usually tell friends ahead of time if we are taking them to a movie or if we need them to help us paint our house. This is not only courteous and automatic; it is socially and psychologically important to let people know what is going to happen and what they are asked to do. The same holds true of students in the classroom.

Possible ways of implementing this principle into the instructional setting are as follows:

1. Verbally introduce the learning activity to the students at the start of the instructional sequence.
2. Write an introduction to the activity on the board or on a handout. Perhaps have a volunteer read it.
3. For secondary students, it may be appropriate to provide a typed list of course and unit goals and objectives.
4. For students in primary grades, it may be most appropriate to inform them at the start of the lesson of the specific skills or types of skills they will possess by the end of the activity. For example, tell first-graders that they will be able to name four types of trees found in and around their school yard by the end of the lesson. Giving young children too much information or information not given in concrete terms may be counterproductive and even anxiety producing.
5. Use a film, record, set of slides, or some object to introduce a learning activity. You may follow this up with a verbal introduction.

Perceived Purpose

In conjunction with task description, by which students are told what they will be doing, *perceived purpose* calls for informing students of the *why* of instruction. When teachers share with students the purpose of the given activity — why it is important, how it may help them, or both — the students typically perform better and participate more than uninformed students. In applying this principle, the teacher attempts to establish in students a "set" or predisposition which increases students' inclination to learn.

This principle is most effective when applied at or toward the beginning of the instructional sequence. The way in which the teacher conveys this purpose to the students is also crucial; the teacher must be sincere and convincing in making introductory remarks about the purpose of the activity. When possible, it is helpful to relate the activity to the personal lives of students, explaining how the activity may positively affect them or what they stand to gain by participating in it. Sample ways of putting forth the purpose or value of a given activity are discussed in the following paragraphs.

1. An example of establishing a set for students learning at the elementary level would be a lesson on emergency situations: using real-life situations drawn from students' experiences and/or from media examples, the class could discuss emergencies in which they may find themselves. This could lead into a lesson focusing on techniques for handling emergencies or on phone numbers to have handy in case of an emergency, or could lead to guest speakers who would address specific procedures to follow in an emergency. The students could clearly see the value of such learning and would undoubtedly have a strong inclination to attend to the information presented.

2. At the secondary level, students in a particular class may be concerned with passing an English proficiency exam in written composition to receive a diploma. To establish a predisposition for attending to a lesson on effective essay writing, the teacher may alert students that they will have the opportunity to simulate the actual test taking required by the district. The students could be told that they will take sample tests, receive individual feedback and assistance on the tests, and work in small groups to practice essay writing. Thus, the value of the lesson is readily apparent to the students, and such an introduction is likely to increase their readiness to participate actively in subsequent lessons.

In some situations it may be difficult to come up with a convincing explanation of how a particular activity may be personally useful or intellectually stimulating. Some students will balk if they are told that understanding algebraic equations will improve their critical thinking skills or that identifying prepositional phrases in a textbook passage will improve their written communication skills. However, if students know that there is a legitimate purpose for the activity and that you personally believe in its importance, it will undoubtedly make the activity somewhat more meaningful or palatable.

Appropriate Practice

Sometimes referred to as "time on task," the principle of *appropriate practice* calls for the provision of ample opportunities for students to practice the behavior designated in the objectives of the activity. A common flaw in learning activities is the failure to build in time and vehicles for students to practice the target behavior. Often a teacher will lecture on a given topic and expect students to grasp the key points and information presented without additional clarification. Support and follow-up are needed if student mastery of such concepts is expected and desired. Students need opportunities to confront the points, often several times, and perhaps in a variety of formats (e.g., written format, small-group discussion, viewing a film, writing a summary). In most cases, as common sense would indicate, practice opportunities should be plentiful, well paced, and well monitored.

The teacher can offer students two basic types of practice: equivalent and analogous. *Equivalent practice* refers to learning opportunities in which students practice the same behavior called for in the instructional objective. For example, if students are to be able to identify the thirteen original U.S. colonies and fill them in on a map, the equivalent practice activities would call for students to work with an outline map of the Eastern United States, use their textbook to identify the colonies, and then label and color in each colony. The final assessment of the given objective would be identical to what the students did as they worked to acquire the historical information.

Analogous practice also calls for students to work toward mastery of the behavior reflected in the instructional objective, but the approach may take a different form. For example, if the objective is for students to design a bird on or out of paper in an art class, analogous practice might allow students to use various mediums, such as watercolor, collage, or pen and ink, in practicing with the characteristics of their subject. In another example, students in small groups in a kindergarten class may be working on the overall objective of creating structures out of blocks. One day students build a castle out of a set of small wooden blocks; another day they build a hospital out of large plastic blocks. Both of these examples show that the students have the opportunity to practice the target behavior, but this type of practice offers different learning conditions for students to gain facility with the behavior.

The following specific examples place this principle in the classroom:

1. True-false tests are often administered by teachers. Although teachers often infer that students simply do not know a missed item, in reality they may be having difficulty with this particular type of test item. Therefore, it would be sound educational practice to provide students with the opportunity to practice taking true-false tests during class instructional time; through subsequent discussions where students justify their answers, they could increase their understanding of how to respond more accurately to this test format.

2. In teaching children a new physical education exercise routine, the teacher may provide two to three minisessions spaced throughout the period when students practice the routine. Perhaps a student volunteer could colead the practice sessions. The children could write down or verbalize the order of the exercises prior to the practice session. Students could work in small groups to practice and critique one another's performance of the routine.

3. In a series of lessons on Haiku poetry, students could have the opportunity to read several published poems and write a number of their own poems. Perhaps they could visit a sharing center where students tape-record or write down and illustrate their original poems. Students could be paired up to quiz one another on the common themes and specific structure and elements of the Haiku.

Knowledge of Results

The principle of *knowledge of results,* sometimes called "instructional feedback," refers to the quick and appropriate response given to students to let them know how they are doing. The sooner students get this information, the better; incorrect information not discovered fast can be internalized, with disastrous repercussions for subsequent learning. The teacher may provide this feedback in a variety of ways, such as an exchange of questions and answers between the teacher and students, exchanging and correcting papers in class, paper correction by an aide or classroom volunteer, or spot-checking and commenting by a teacher who circulates around the classroom. The tone used by the teacher to communicate the knowledge of results is of primary importance. A spirit of openness to questions and an air of accessibility and supportiveness encourage students to seek such feedback. When applied consistently and thoroughly this principle markedly improves student achievement and often attitude.

Examples of the knowledge-of-results principle applied to the classroom are as follows:

1. In small reading groups, the students read the assigned story silently. Then students go around in a circle, telling each major event of the story in sequence. Students monitor and correct one another.

2. The classroom aide corrects the math tests while students complete a questionnaire and play a math game; students receive their tests to take home by the end of the period and are to rework any problems missed on the test.

3. The teacher circulates through the class as the students work on their mobiles, giving suggestions, encouragement, and assistance as needed.

4. Essay tests provide a challenge to the teacher trying to apply this principle, especially because of the immediacy problem. A way to handle this might be to provide samples of a superior response on the exam, of an average response, and of a below-average response (by withholding students' names, providing teacher-generated responses, or using responses from previous years to fit the categories). This set could be distributed as students leave class on the day of the exam, or on the following day when the questions and students' responses are still fresh in the minds of the students. Ideally, the sample responses could be discussed with the students for more thorough clarification.

Motivation

Although the concept of *motivation* overlaps with several other learning principles, we have chosen to present it separately so that key concepts of classroom motivation may be highlighted.

A traditional way of viewing motivation is that of capturing the attention of the students. An example of this would be a teacher introducing a unit on household pets by bringing in a live hamster. However, while sparking the interest of learners to increase their receptivity to a new area of study is conducive to learning, other aspects of motivation need to be incorporated into one's teaching repertoire.

Effective learning also requires that the students' interest and attention to the task at hand be sustained. When students are able to maintain a high level of interest and involvement in learning, then *intrinsic motivation* has been developed. Intrinsic motivation refers to the internal sense of satisfaction derived from involvement in activity and directing it to its completion. Valuing learning for the sake of learning and deciding that the effort is worth expending are perhaps the most important attitudes a student can acquire in school. They will lead to a more thorough mastery of content and will have an impact on the student's self-concept and future learning.

Intrinsic motivation of students would be demonstrated in a classroom where reading for personal enjoyment is evident. The students voluntarily choose to do free reading when they complete their regularly assigned work, simply for the pleasure derived from reading; no reward, check mark, or grade influences their decision to read.

Extrinsic motivation, on the other hand, refers to learning situations in which the student participates to achieve some results, such as a grade or a token. This form of motivation obviously has its place in the classroom and may often prove effective in keeping students on task. Caution should be taken when using extrinsic motivators with students so that the students do not come to rely solely on receiving such rewards. If students are gradually weaned of such extrinsic rewards, it is sometimes possible, and certainly desirable, to create a state of intrinsic motivation.

An example of extrinsic motivation operating at the elementary level would be a classroom where the children are given a token upon completing each math activity in a unit. The tokens would be saved and redeemed at some future time, perhaps for a special reward or freetime activities. At the secondary level, extrinsic motivation might be evident as students work toward receiving an "A" in their history class, having been given the guidelines for receiving an "A." Some members of the class will then follow the guidelines to earn that desired grade. While they may be interested in the course content, at least part of their motivation is attached to the extrinsic reward of a "good" grade.

The following classroom conditions serve to increase motivation in the classroom: classroom atmosphere, student involvement, ensuring success, and transfer and retention.

Classroom atmosphere. Generally, students respond and perform well when the teacher is supportive and helpful throughout the learning sequence; also, student motivation is often positively affected by teacher vitality and sincere enthusiasm for the content being taught. However, in some cases and with some students, it is most effective to be more stern, withholding positive feedback until the task is completed. This requires that the teacher be able to carefully assess the learning atmosphere in the classroom and effectively read the students. The atmosphere should usually be comfortable and supportive, but the motivating possibilities derived from having a range within which to deal with students can yield positive results.

Student involvement.   If the subject matter in the classroom is related to the personal lives and interests of the students, the learning process will usually be more involving and motivating for the students. For example, if popular music is used as the theme when presenting parts of speech, students may be more apt to actively participate in the learning activities. Again, this requires a teacher who is attuned to the students and is willing to slightly modify the lessons to accommodate the interests and areas of personal involvement of the students.

Ensuring success.   It is common knowledge that most students respond positively when they succeed. While some failure situations certainly may motivate some learners to work harder, it is generally more motivating to succeed. Therefore, the teacher should build into the learning sequence as many opportunities as possible for the success of all of the students. This may require that the teacher provide extra reinforcement and guidance; however, the payoff will be apparent as students become more willing to take risks and devote their attention to the task over time.

For further discussion of principles of motivation which can enhance learning and interaction in the classroom, see Madeline Hunter's book, *Mastery Teaching.*

Transfer and Retention

Transfer of learning from one situation to another is sometimes called "learning to learn." *Retention* refers to the capacity to remember learned information over time. Both of these are vital learning principles for readily apparent reasons.

What a teacher emphasizes in the classroom is generally indicative of the principle of transfer in operation. For instance, if a teacher stresses neat handwriting during spelling, written composition, and social studies, then it is likely that students will transfer this learning (behavior) across a variety of instructional situations.

In a kindergarten classroom, the teacher may want to encourage sharing behavior. Therefore, the teacher would set up a variety of situations in which group sharing and cooperation are called for, such as (1) small-group playtime in the class kitchen where students share utensils and appliances to prepare an imaginary meal; (2) small-group art project in which paints and brushes must be shared to complete a group mural; and (3) a small-group social studies session in which children share magazines and scissors to create a multicultural mobile. In providing activities in which students see the benefit of sharing and exhibit this behavior to complete group tasks, the teacher increases the likelihood that sharing behavior will be transferred to other learning and social settings, such as sharing playground equipment, sharing snacks, or sharing blocks during free time.

Another type of "learning to learn" behavior may be the application of problem-solving skills in high school, whereby the math teacher and the economics teacher call for problem-solving skills in their courses. In the transfer of deductive logic, for example, which may be a goal in high school geometry, the teacher would not solely rely on the theorems to promote this goal. The teacher would not assume that students automatically glean the deductive reasoning process simply by learning and modeling the proofs. For transfer to occur, the teacher must signpost and continually highlight the process which is being used — in this case, deductive logic. In all cases, teachers ensure a higher level of transfer among students when they emphasize what students are to transfer in the learning sequence.

The single most important factor in retention is the degree of initial learning; in other words, how effectively the information is presented and learned initially is the best indicator of how well the information will be retained. Studies reveal that learning by rote is not as effective as when material is applied. Also, material presented at the beginning and at the end of a unit of learning (activity, lecture, lesson, etc.) is better remembered than information presented in the middle of such a sequence.

The following examples of applying transfer and retention to the classroom are provided:

1. In a history course at the secondary level, an example of how to increase student retention would be a strong captivating preliminary lesson introducing World War II. A graphic film depicting the concentration camps, posters of American troops overseas, and patriotic songs from the era could be employed to elicit an emotional response in the students. Initial lessons could focus on facts and events in the war, which students would compare to current international situations; these lessons would differ from assignments in which students memorize dates of early battles and names of random military leaders. The combination of evoking a visceral response from students and showing how historical events apply to their personal lives would undoubtedly lead to greater retention of learning.

2. An example of the use of imagery to enhance retention of learning at the elementary level would be the use of birds' nests and large colored posters of birds to introduce a science unit. The use of such engaging visual imagery would most likely increase the processing of information related to bird life because children would be provided with mental images on which to draw during subsequent lessons.

Example at the Primary Level. Real-life experiences or simulation experiences also provide an effective means by which to increase retention. An example at the primary level would be the use of an aquarium in the classroom when studying underwater life. Students could be given an artificial ecosystem with which to interact and view. Such real-life experiences enhance initial learning and provide mental images from which the student can draw at a later stage of instruction.

In general, most instructional sequences rely on a written or spoken message to convey information to students. It is essential to augment the verbal message with a visual image whenever possible. Providing opportunities for students to create a visual image or providing a pictorial representation helps them retain the material better. Magazines, newspapers, and television apply this basic principle of learning in the everyday communication of societal information; the visual images used in such media often carry the greatest impact of the conveyed message. Likewise, the increased use of visuals in the classroom would lead to more solid concept formation as well as better retention of ideas and information.

Elementary classrooms generally provide students with more visuals than other levels, while higher education typically provides the least. Perhaps because of the concrete level of operations of elementary-age students, teachers have intuitively incorporated visual stimuli more rigorously into the learning environment. Traditional examples of visuals at this level include the cardboard alphabet often found above the chalkboard, a large monthly calendar, and bulletin boards with a variety of colors and shapes. Teachers often read stories aloud and show the illustrations which accompany the text, and children may participate in "show and tell." Examples of ways to expand the use of visuals at the elementary level include:

- showing color slides to enhance a lesson (animals, geographical locations, etc.)
- using three-dimensional models to augment a lecture (body organs, model-buildings, etc.)
- incorporating drawings and photographs into learning centers (photo-story starters, make-your-own vocabulary flashcards with words and drawings, etc.)

At the secondary level, visual reinforcement can strengthen student learning and increase understanding of materials. A overreliance on textbook reading and teacher-presented lecture creates a void of potentially useful visual images. Examples, by secondary subject areas, in which the provision of visual stimulation may be appropriate include:

- English: Using color slides, photographs, art prints, and drawings when studying a specific novel, poem, or play. *The Great Gatsby* could be introduced by showing slides of the fashions and fads of the time period of the novel.

- Math: Incorporating charts and illustrations of mathematical concepts into lessons. Graphing, creating number lines, and drawing and labeling geometric shapes can be done individually and in small groups.
- Social studies: Including films, photographs, posters, and slides with lectures. Students can create murals and collages to present historical events and social trends.

Teachers will find significant benefits in incorporating visuals into the instructional sequence. Using a variety of resources can lighten the teacher's burden of personally providing such visuals; students, libraries, museums, local businesses, and agencies can provide a wealth of materials to promote the visualization of concepts in the classroom.

Individual Differentiation

Each learner in the classroom is unique in personality, areas of interests, and motivation to learn, to name but a few variables. In addition, learners have individual differences in how they learn. Most people view learning differences as a preference for using a certain *learning modality*. While this is important, it is only a piece of the puzzle in the determination of individual differences in the classroom.

The basic learning modalities, or means by which learners take in information to be processed, are auditory (by listening); visual (through seeing); and kinesthetic (through touching and muscular response). Research has shown that most people typically rely on one of these modalities more than the others when learning. For example, when some people learn to spell a new word, they say the word to themselves and they spell it out loud or silently to remember the spelling; this is an example of auditory learning. Other learners may visualize the new word, then write it several times to get a mental image of the way the correctly spelled word should look; this is an example of visual learning. For a kinesthetic learner, the process of cutting the word out of sandpaper and touching the rough letters as the completed word is said and seen would be a way to process the correct spelling. While the sandpaper is simply an example of a way to accommodate to this type of learner, it is indicative of the necessary ingredient of providing a tactile dimension to accompany the learning process.

In addition to understanding the significance of learning modalities in the classroom, it is vital to be familiar with right- and left-brain learning and verbal and quantitative preferences in learning.

Right- and left-brain learning refers to the fact that the brain is double; each hemisphere is capable of functioning independently, each in a manner different from the other. Left-brain learners (those who are right-brain dominant when learning) are generally verbal learners; they rely on the verbal processes of reading, speaking, and writing and on calculating while they acquire new knowledge. Conversely, right-brain learners use synthesis when processing information and take a holistic view of the learning, as contrasted with left-brain learners who process information sequentially. Although a learner may use both sides of the brain when learning, generally one hemisphere is more dominant than the other.

Example at the Primary Level.   Applying the concept of right- and left-brain learning to primary grades, the teacher may ask students studying music to write the names of their favorite instrument after listening to a story about instruments in the orchestra; this calls for left-brain processing, of which the process of verbal learning is an essential part. Right-brain processing would be promoted when students listen to a recording of a minuet and are asked to draw a picture in response to the music; this activity calls for a holistic response to the music, through listening and artistic expression.

An example of right- and left-brain learning may be drawn from the teaching of economics. Let us take the concept of demand, which is "wants backed by the ability (willingness) to pay." It refers to the way consumers believe they will act in purchasing products at some specific time. Learning this concept in the classroom, left-brain learners would be able to understand the concept through an oral or written definition and example: "As the price of a good or service goes down, the amount people are willing to buy tends to go up." However, the concept would be much more clear to right-brain learners through the use of a graphical depiction of the concept (see Figure 2–1).

Another distinction between learners is that of *verbal versus quantitative learning styles.* Verbal learners, of course, rely most heavily on written material and verbalized explanations of concepts, while quantitative learners are more comfortable with symbols. In math, for example, some students prefer to be presented with a clear-cut mathematical formula, while others require a verbal explanation to understand the concept. In some cases, a confounding factor may mask the learner's innate ability; sometimes the learner is symbol shy, not feeling comfortable with symbols. These individuals often have a quantitative aptitude, but their personalities are people-oriented. Therefore, their proclivity leads them toward verbal interaction, when in reality they are very capable of handling the quantitative style.

Having looked into learning modalities, right- and left-brain learning, and verbal versus quantitative learning, it is essential to apply this information to the role of teacher. Because completely accurate assessments of all learners to determine learning style and preference are difficult to find and extremely time-consuming to administer, it seems fitting that teachers incorporate teaching approaches which combine the requisite features of the various learning styles. Aside from practicality, integrating verbal and visual presentations during instruction has been shown to strengthen the learning of both types of learners and aid them in future learning.

It is also desirable, when appropriate to the subject matter, to present information both verbally and quantitatively. Learners may then process information using these diverse mental processes.

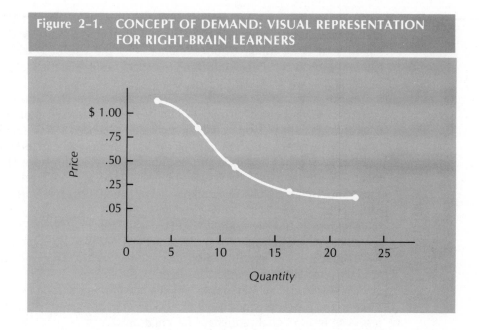

Figure 2-1. CONCEPT OF DEMAND: VISUAL REPRESENTATION FOR RIGHT-BRAIN LEARNERS

Such accommodation to individual styles of learning may be found in many classrooms, even in those classrooms where teachers would not be able to provide an underlying rationale but have intuitively found such practices effective. In conclusion, it is sound educational practice to combine ways of presenting information to students so that certain students are not lacking understanding because of the mode of presentation.

Developmental Awareness

Both children and adults go through developmental stages. However, children are not miniature adults in terms of their development; they go through these stages at their own rate. In other words, development is qualitative; great leaps forward are followed by a period of integration rather than by step-by-step changes in degree. It is especially important for beginning teachers to take this into account. Students have their own inner timetable for staying in place or moving on to the next stage. Generally, the onset of each stage is predetermined hierarchically, but effective and timely environmental stimulation is needed for each stage to blossom and unfold on schedule.

Stages of development for children have been delineated primarily from the work of Jean Piaget. From ages two to seven is the *preoperational stage;* this represents a breakthrough in the child's ability to use language. The child is capable of using symbols, or words, to represent reality. However, at this stage children are not capable of sustained, systematic thought. A child in the preoperational stage of development would be able to acquire language very rapidly and think things through mentally by the use of verbal symbols. Generally, behavior is egocentric and nonsocial, at least in the early phases of this stage.

In the stage of *concrete operations,* covering the years from seven to eleven, children become capable of limited logical thought, but only when manipulatable concrete materials are provided. Children at this stage can perform tasks involving seriation (putting things in order) and can focus on more than one aspect of a perceptual field simultaneously. At this stage of development, children are able to assume or understand another's point of view. Also, children are able to problem solve when concrete information is provided.

Children ages eleven and older, in the stage of *formal operations,* develop the ability to reason logically and abstractly. They can test hypotheses, and their thought is no longer limited to concrete reality. They can play with abstract possibilities and reflect on their own thinking.

These developmental stages provide an important framework for the teacher and have tremendous implications when designing effective and appropriate instructional sequences for children.

For a more in-depth analysis and application of stages of development, see *Piaget's Theory of Cognitive and Affective Development* by Barry Wadsworth.

LESSON AND UNIT PLANNING

Armed with a thorough working knowledge of goal and objective writing, preassessment, task analysis, and principles of learning, the teacher puts this knowledge into operation when designing written instructional plans. The two main types of written plans for classroom use are lesson plans and unit plans.

A *lesson plan* is typically developed for a single instructional sequence, usually presented in one class session. The instructional objective(s) which the teacher plans to promote in the lesson forms the core of this written plan. The other elements of the plan deal with (1) the logistics of presenting the lesson, that is, needed instructional materials, procedural steps, time allocation; (2) the application of learning principles (motivation); and (3) the use of evaluation techniques. Although not specifically called for here, all major learning principles should be considered in planning the lesson and incorporated when the lesson is actually implemented (see ''Principles of Learning,'' Chapter Two). There are a variety of lesson plan formats available; some districts have specific, uniform outlines to follow for lesson planning.

We have selected an outline containing seven key elements of a lesson plan which would, depending upon effective delivery, yield a strong and well-designed instructional sequence. These lesson plan components are listed and described here:

1. *Instructional objectives.* — The particular objective(s) to be covered during the class period(s) are described precisely and operationally.
2. *Materials.* — The instructional materials which will be used during the lesson are explained in terms of the purpose and way in which they will be integrated into the lesson.
3. *Motivation.* — A description is given of the way the teacher intends to introduce and/or capture interest when initiating the lesson. The plan may include other aspects of motivation, such as how success will be ensured and any motivators to be used during the course of the instruction.
4. *Procedure.* — Steps in the instructional sequence will be provided which include the role of the teacher and the possible roles of the students. Sample questions to be used during the sequence may be provided. This element contains both teacher and student behaviors/activities during instruction.
5. *Time estimates.* — A careful notation of the amount of time scheduled for each phase of the learning sequence should be provided in the plan; this is helpful in pacing the instruction.
6. *Evaluation.* — A framework of questions and topics with which to evaluate the strengths and weaknesses of the lesson is needed. An opportunity for students to evaluate the lesson may also be included.
7. *Independent work and follow-up.* — If included, follow-up assignments should be explained in the plan. This includes activities such as visitations to learning centers and libraries, homework assignments based on the lesson's objectives, or a group activity which will occur later in the week to review the objectives.

Samples of an elementary and secondary lesson plan may be found in Chapter 9.

An instructional unit is a series of unified instructional sequences presented over time. A unit may last a few days or an entire semester but usually is presented over the course of several weeks.

There are two major categories of teaching units: interdisciplinary units and subject area units. *Interdisciplinary units* integrate more than one subject area; for example, an interdisciplinary unit on whales may combine objectives from science, English, and art. A *subject area unit,* on the other hand, stays within a specific content or subject area; examples would be a history unit on the major wars in American history or an English unit on the American short story.

As with lesson plans, the goals and objectives are the core building blocks of the unit; these need to be extensive enough to support the ongoing thematic instruction.

The key elements of an instructional unit are listed and described here:

Background information. This section should introduce the unit in terms of the basic educational philosophy on which the unit is based. For example, the unit, based upon a humanistic philosophy of education, may be intended to strengthen the self-concept of learners. Depending upon the author of the unit, this may be a brief paragraph or a more lengthy description. Also, this section should contain a brief description of the learners for whom the unit has been designed and a brief description of the school. This is important not only to the new teacher but to the seasoned veteran as well because units are used many times, and the previous information is necessary if and when the unit is to be adapted to a new set of learners in a different educational setting.

Unit description. This section should contain a brief explanation of the topic of the unit and the reason the unit was developed. Also, the complete set of goals and objectives for the unit should be contained in this section. The objectives should be stated in precise and measurable terms.

Instructional plan. This section focuses on the actual learning sequences planned for the unit. It should contain:

- A task analysis of the unit. This would include a description of the requisite baseline behavior(s) of the learners, determined by preassessment, and the intermediate steps toward the achievement of the behaviors targeted for the unit.
- A schedule of the activities designed for the unit on a weekly basis.
- A description of the major activities found in the unit. It should be a concise, paragraph description highlighting the purpose of each activity, the basic instructional strategy to be used, and the length of time intended for each activity.
- The sample daily lesson plan should be a representative lesson plan from the unit, using the aforementioned lesson plan outline. In addition, some teachers may wish to include a backup lesson plan in this section in case there is an unforeseen problem in implementing one of the planned lessons; for example, in case a speaker who is scheduled to visit does not arrive, the backup lesson, preplanned and adapted to the overall unit, would be optimal.

Resources and instructional materials. This section includes key resources used in designing the unit and materials available for implementation.

- Student materials and texts to be used during the unit.
- Audiovisual resources and field trips incorporated into the unit.

- Additional ideas related to the unit, including bulletin boards, learning centers, and sample worksheets.
- Bibliography of all resources used to compile the unit.

Evaluation procedure. This section provides an explanation (and examples, when appropriate) of evaluation procedures applied to the unit, including preassessment and formative unit evaluation.

- Preassessment of the unit should be explained. This will be somewhat similar in content to the section on task analysis, when assessing entry behavior is discussed. Instruments used in preassessment may include observation checklists, interview forms, and other relevant documents to be employed by the teacher for the initial assessment of students.
- Formative evaluation procedures to be used during the unit. Also called criterion checks, these are the indicators teachers will look for to reflect student learning and acquisition of objectives during the unit. In addition to describing the actual means of such ongoing evaluation, any sample assessment instruments and recordkeeping forms may be included.
- Unit evaluation to provide a teacher and student assessment of the perceived success of the unit. The unit evaluation should incorporate sample questions which analyze the strengths and weaknesses of the unit in terms of its original set of objectives. Sample assessment instruments, recordkeeping forms, and provisions for student feedback should be included.

Samples of an elementary unit and critique and a secondary unit and critique may be found in Chapter Nine.

CLASSROOM MANAGEMENT

A critical aspect of successful classroom management consists of appropriate and effective disciplinary approaches and techniques. One's educational philosophy and basic assumption concerning learners generally dictate the disciplinary strategies employed in the classroom. Occasionally, however, a teacher new to a school may find a school-wide discipline system in operation. Then, if the teacher accepts the system, it becomes a matter of receiving training in the method and implementing it.

More typically, teachers individually select and implement a particular approach or set of approaches which incorporate their personal style of discipline. Some teachers are most comfortable with a structured model, while others prefer to have a repertoire of strategies to use depending upon the student and the particular situation.

In this section we will present a sampling of three models of discipline. Each model will be described and applied to the classroom. These models do not constitute the entire range of available systems of discipline but serve to highlight contrasting methods available. In addition, we will provide a list of techniques which do not comprise a particular model but may be helpful for teachers more eclectic in their classroom management approach.

Before discussing approaches for managing behavior, we would like to mention some guidelines which generally promote a productive and positive environment, thus eliminating many potential problems:

- Provide a stimulating and appropriate learning environment for students which takes into account their personal interests and learning styles.
- Use a variety of instructional strategies in the classroom; use novelty to break up routines.
- Allow students to generate guidelines for proper classroom conduct, thus building in ownership and increasing awareness of personal responsibility for one's actions.
- Treat students with respect and kindness, express concern for student welfare, and provide opportunities for success in the classroom.

The three models of classroom discipline we will present are (1) behavior modification, (2) assertive discipline, and (3) the psychoanalytic approach. (See Figure 2–2.)

A behavior modification approach to discipline, based primarily on the work of B. F. Skinner, asserts that behavior is shaped by the consequences of that behavior. When reinforcers follow behavior, that behavior will tend to be repeated. Punishment and negative reinforcement tend to weaken behavior. In this approach, the *causes* of inappropriate behavior are not of concern. Rather, the focus is on the observable behavior of students and the reinforcers applied to that behavior. Control in the classroom, then, is external to the student because reinforcers are given or taken away by the teacher. Proponents of this approach attempt to "shape" student behavior by providing or withholding extrinsic rewards. Among the types of reinforcers used are (1) activity-based — free time, special activity; (2) visual reinforcement — special stickers placed on work, charted scores or grades; and (3) social-based — verbal acknowledgment or nonverbal message, generally by the teacher.

In implementing a behavior modification system, clear and consistent guidelines of desired student behavior must be established and communicated to students. Reinforcers are determined for use with students. In some cases, teachers may use tangible rewards, such as tokens, candy, or prizes, as reinforcers. Sometimes, behavior contracts are set up with built-in rewards and reinforcers. Behavior modification calls for a systematic and con-

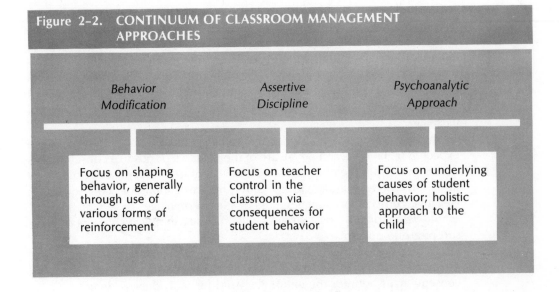

Figure 2-2. CONTINUUM OF CLASSROOM MANAGEMENT APPROACHES

Behavior Modification

Assertive Discipline

Psychoanalytic Approach

Focus on shaping behavior, generally through use of various forms of reinforcement

Focus on teacher control in the classroom via consequences for student behavior

Focus on underlying causes of student behavior; holistic approach to the child

sistent approach for identifying problem behaviors and replacing them with appropriate or target behaviors through the use of negative and positive reinforcers and punishment.

Behavior modification techniques appear most effective when applied to nonacademic behaviors in the classroom. For diminishing disruptive behavior, such as calling out without raising one's hand or getting out of one's seat without permission, withholding teacher attention often seems to work. When the teacher reinforces positive behaviors, students exhibiting unsatisfactory behavior tend to improve their behavior to match that of their peers. However, research has shown that behavior modification techniques are generally less successful in promoting academic achievement. A key factor here is the emphasis on extrinsic rewards in behavior modification approaches. Intrinsic motivation, by which students pursue knowledge and demonstrate positive behavior because they choose to and because it is personally rewarding, is the ultimate goal in education. When using this approach, one should keep in mind the long-term effects of using extrinsic motivators and work to diminish the teacher's and students' need for them in the learning environment.

The second model of discipline we will present is that of assertive discipline, sometimes called the Canter Model (after its originators, Lee and Marlene Canter). This approach advocates teacher assertiveness in the classroom. In addition, students are held responsible for their behavior and must face the consequences of their behavioral choices. The model holds that specific rules must be established in the classroom, with clear and appropriate consequences for infraction and compliance. Although students' self-control is often an ultimate goal of this approach, teacher interaction, intervention, and monitoring are used extensively. Teachers are to make clear, direct, and assertive statements regarding expected behavior and are to follow up such statements with predetermined corresponding actions or consequences. Verbal limit-setting provides students with specific messages from the teacher about what their behavior should be. Adding a nonverbal message, such as a gesture or physical proximity, can strengthen this verbal message.

A basic premise of this model of discipline is that students know what the expected behavior is and are aware of the negative or positive consequences which result from their behavior. It is then a matter of a student deciding how to behave, knowing ahead of time the corresponding consequences. Negative consequences may be loss of special privileges or serving an after-school detention. Positive consequences may be a certificate of merit or some sort of group reward.

Canter and Canter also suggest that teachers create discipline plans, similar to lesson plans, which identify desired behaviors, interventions, and consequences both for the entire class and for individual students.

Assertive discipline techniques appear to be most effective when the teacher communicates the underlying concepts clearly and is a consistent implementer of the system. When students are clear about expected behaviors in the classroom and have actively shared in establishing group rules, a true linkage between the initial communication of the system and its ultimate, successful implementation tends to develop. It appears to be less effective when used by more spontaneous teachers who do not consistently follow the procedures of the system and in classes where students are nonverbal and nonparticipatory, thus breaking down a feeling of ownership and personal commitment to the program. For a more detailed look at this approach, refer to *Assertive Discipline: A Take-Charge Approach for Today's Educator* by Canter and Canter.

The third method of discipline in the classroom is the psychoanalytic approach. Here, the teacher strives to uncover the person's past to determine the cause of the misbehavior. Sometimes classified as a humanistic approach to discipline, this method advocates dealing with the whole person and trying to discover underlying motivation and attitudes which affect the ongoing behavior. The teacher is more of a counselor than a rule setter or reward giver in such settings and strives to determine the emotional, social, and psychological characteristics and needs of each student. A major goal is to help students arrive at insights into their behavior patterns and take responsibility for healthy change.

A major influence in this approach to classroom interaction is Carl Rogers, a noted psychotherapist, who has applied his work and theories to the classroom setting. He stresses the interdependence of one's emotional state and attitudes and one's intellectuality; he believes in unifying these facets of oneself to increase one's sense of wholeness and self-directedness.

Active listening, whereby the teacher listens receptively and openly without judging the content of the message or labeling the student, is advocated. Through such interaction, the teacher serves as a role model of an empathetic, supportive individual who helps students move toward self-acceptance and a healthy self-concept. To promote such personal growth and increase the students' sense of trust and worth, the teacher may hold one-on-one interviews or talk sessions with the students or meet privately with them before or after school. Parents and school counseling staff may also become involved in some of these sessions.

Proponents of this approach generally agree that some training in psychoanalysis, counseling, or both is warranted before using this approach in the classroom. Because teachers do not simply focus on immediate behavior and tangible actions, they must learn how to communicate and interact with students to determine motivation behind and causes underlying their behavior.

This approach seems to be most effective when the teacher is viewed as nonpunitive and genuinely supportive of the student as a "whole" person. When a closed and punitive climate is coupled with a seemingly nurturing teacher, there is a discordance in the classroom. If a teacher is truly comfortable with the psychoanalytic approach, is skillful in communicating with students openly and nonjudgmentally, and is able to set up the learning environment to allow for feelings, emotions, and attitudes, then a positive and productive climate can be the result.

These three models of discipline form a representative continuum of potential management styles and systems. One's personal and professional attitudes and beliefs toward student behavior will greatly influence the selection of such a system in the classroom.

In turning now to a more generalized look at disciplinary techniques, an outline of teacher attitudes and behaviors is provided, along with key support areas. These may be used singularly or in conjunction with a given model of discipline. (See Figure 2–3).

In summary, managing the behavior of students or assisting them in managing their own behavior is a challenging and on-going task for the classroom teacher. In general, if boredom and frustration levels can be minimized and an engaging, supportive learning environment provided, students will choose to participate actively and positively.

TEACHER-LED INSTRUCTIONAL TECHNIQUES

There is no question that the role of the teacher is of primary importance in constructing, implementing, and assessing instruction and learning in the classroom. Teacher characteristics, attitudes, and personality have been shown to have a significant impact on student learning, with both positive and negative outcomes. A teacher may have excellent planning skills, may

Figure 2–3. SUGGESTED ATTITUDES, BEHAVIORS, AND SUPPORTS FOR EFFECTIVE CLASSROOM RAPPORT AND MANAGEMENT

Teacher Attitudes	Teacher Behaviors	Teacher Supports
Students are responsible for their behavior and capable of responsible behavior	Communicate clearly to students; use "I" messages whenever possible	Classroom aids/ volunteers
Good behavior promotes an environment conducive to learning	Use proximity to student and sometimes touching to bring student back to task	Peer monitoring/ Small-group work
The teacher should identify with the student— be on the same team as the student	Change seating assignment	School administrators
	Initiate behavior contracts for individuals	Parent input
	Use humor and warmth to deflect anger when appropriate	
	Give students choices when possible	
	Role-model good behavior; treat students as you want to be treated	
	Ignore student's action(s) when appropriate to do so	
	Restructure the lesson	
	Listen to students; discuss situation	
	Remind students of predetermined class rules	

create exemplary lessons on paper, and may have a veritable showroom for a classroom and yet fail to create successful learning experiences for students. It is therefore important to look at the actions and behaviors of the teacher to provide a personalized profile of teachers who succeed or fail in reaching their students.

One major area of teacher behavior to consider is interpersonal communication. Because the didactic, or lecture method, is still one of the most widely used instructional approaches, the act of communication and the teacher's role within this act are of primary importance. The teacher functions in the classroom primarily as a communicator, whether lecturing, giving directions for a test, or explaining a homework assignment, and teacher communication comprises a special set of requisite skills for maximum effectiveness.

In communicating during didactic instruction, the teacher usually is the primary *source* of the stimuli, and each individual in the class is a *receiver*. The message is primarily the verbal manifestation of the process of communication but in a larger sense could refer to the totality of stimuli transmitted to the receiver. Thus, the message includes nonverbal as well as verbal communication. Any *response* to a symbolic stimulus must by definition involve some form of cognition by which the receiver decodes the message. The receiver's response may be primarily cognitive or primarily emotional. The response then acts as feedback to the sender, signaling whether the message has been correctly received or whether it needs repetition or modification. The process of communication is circular, with various forms of feedback between sender and receiver affecting the communication.

Given this basic introduction to a model of communication, we can look at communication in the classroom from the point of view of breakdowns which may occur in the act of communication and corresponding remedies to these breakdowns. Communication may be interrupted because of an interfering factor; such interference, or communication breakdown, refers to any physical or psychological factor which impedes communication from the point of view of the receiver, each student.

Breakdowns in communication can be found in the sender (teacher), the message (lesson), or the receiver (student). Each source of potential breakdown and its explanation follow.

The Message Sender: The Teacher

The communicator may have a *negative antecedent ethos* which inhibits the transmittal of the message. *Ethos* (Greek: character) refers to the personal image conveyed by the speaker, for example, poise, psychological dominance (feeling in control of the situation), disposition. A teacher's antecedent ethos is the image projected before the message is transmitted, that is, prior to actually teaching the lesson. The students' immediate reaction toward the speaker may be so negative that they tune out the teacher.

The teacher also may convey a *negative manifest ethos*. Manifest ethos refers to the image projected *while* speaking. The gestalt of the teacher's attitudes and personality may elicit such a negative reaction from a listener that the listener ceases concentrating on the speaker and message. For example, a teacher might inadvertently communicate to the student-listener that the teacher finds the subject boring; thus, the student-listener will most likely respond to that implicit communication by shifting attention away from the bored teacher and message.

The Message: The Lesson

The vocal quality of delivery may inhibit effective communication of the message. The teacher may speak too quickly or in a monotone. The teacher may have poor enunciation or diction or speak too softly or mumble. The teacher may exhibit one, several, or, conceivably, all of these problems simultaneously. The lack of this type of communication skills in the speaker often results in listeners losing interest and allowing their minds to wander. Another factor of delivery is *mannerisms*, both physical and verbal, which impede message communication. Verbal mannerisms include repeating words or phrases, for example, ''um,'' excessively. Physical mannerisms include pacing, making nervous or repetitive hand gestures, clicking ballpoint pens, and many other actions. Mannerisms detract from the message and make the lessons tiresome. This tiresomeness manifests itself in students' nonattentive behavior, such as doodling, looking around the room, or misbehaving.

The teacher may deviate from the main core of the lesson. The logical progression of ideas may be interrupted when the teacher becomes sidetracked onto an unrelated idea. These *digressions* may become prolonged or recurrent. When the teacher returns to the core material and gets back on track, some students will not be following.

Lack of message clarity may also result in communication breakdown. The message may be ambiguous because of conflicting verbal and nonverbal messages or because of vagueness in the language. Language may contain words or phrases that have multiple interpretations. While searching for the proper meaning, the student is not listening to the rest of the message. Simultaneous verbal and nonverbal communications may convey inconsistent messages, creating confusion. Such is the case with the teacher who communicates verbally, ''You may disagree with my opinion, as long as your answer is well supported,'' but who simultaneously communicates nonverbally that a student who disagrees will be penalized.

The *level of abstraction* may detract from the clarity of the message. The teacher may employ verbal symbols unknown to the students or combine them in unusual ways. The result is that students find the lesson over their heads. Even when the ideas presented are within the students' cognitive ability, the mode of expression may cause communication breakdown if the teacher assumes the students are more familiar with the subject or have a better understanding of it than is actually the case. This type of communication breakdown often appears in the sciences; for example, a chemistry teacher may explain an experiment on the assumption that students can decode the terms and notations as quickly as the instructor is progressing. Examples can also be found in the social sciences, such as political science, where students are constantly grappling with new terminology. The teacher's presentation may be faster than the students' ability to decode the nomenclature and understand each idea, for example, "Wealth maximization seeks to limit nonreciprocal risk." The teacher may progress to explaining a new idea before the students have interpreted "wealth maximization" and "nonreciprocal risk."

The Message Receiver: The Student

In any listening situation *diversion of attention* is a common communication problem. The student may focus attention on a physical object, such as a picture or an individual. During this period the student has ignored the message being communicated.

Every listener is subject to *concentration fatigue*. The degree of fatigue will depend on the widely divergent individual concentration spans. When fatigue occurs, the listener will decode the communication symbols only selectively or randomly or may stop decoding entirely. As a result, the message the student receives may be incomplete or even distorted.

Attention may be diverted from the communication by *spontaneous thought linkage*. The listener will spontaneously recall an unpaid bill or a letter the listener forgot to mail. One thought leads to another; for example, the letter not mailed may concern a trip home, which may lead to thoughts about the family, which in turn results in thinking about vacation plans . . . The result is temporary interference with the message.

Perception of the environment affects the listener's ability to receive the communication. This includes both physical and psychological perceptions. If physically uncomfortable (e.g., cold or sitting in a hard chair), the listener will be unable to focus full attention on the speaker and message. Similarly, if the listener is psychologically ill-at-ease in the environment, for example, in a social group experienced as intimidating, the listener cannot fully concentrate on the message being communicated by the teacher.

The preceding communication breakdowns may adversely affect instruction in the classroom. The following suggestions serve to ameliorate the effects of communication breakdown.

To remedy a negative antecedent ethos, conveyed by a teacher prior to speaking, the teacher may attempt to level with the students. For example, the teacher may say, "As you may have noticed, I look pretty grouchy this morning, and I am. I was up all night with my sick daughter. Bear with me, and I'm sure I'll be myself in a little while." Also, studies have revealed that teachers who try not to take themselves too seriously and occasionally poke fun at themselves can sometimes improve the problems of a negative antecedent ethos.

A teacher who can improve delivery skills will obviously be able to retain the attention of listeners for longer periods of time. Frequent variations in volume, rate, pitch, and inflection make the message appear more interesting. A reduction in speed makes the decoding process easier for the listener. Also, an increase in animation may improve the effectiveness of delivery.

To alleviate some of the effects of digression, it is helpful to label a digression as such — "Let me digress a moment." When ready to get back on track, the instructor might inform the class that this is what is happening.

Ambiguity arising from the language used by the teacher can be clarified by the teacher's defining any term that may not be a part of the students' active vocabulary. When in doubt, *define*.

When the level of abstraction is resulting in loss of the listeners, the teacher may increase the number of concrete examples. In the explanation of a process, each step should be included and clarified, even those which may appear obvious.

Since diversion of attention, concentration fatigue, and spontaneous thought linkage are common to all students in their role as listeners, the following principles could prove helpful in diminishing the effects of these breakdowns:

1. *Repetition.* — Tell the students what you are going to tell them, then tell them, and then remind them of what you have told them is a useul procedure to follow. Repeating key concepts and reminding students what is important in the lesson serves to reduce the effects of lapses of attention in the classroom.

2. *Summarization.* — Frequent summarizations of material and concepts, both from the teacher and the students, will help remind students what is being presented. Such summarizations allow for listeners to adjust and refocus their listening.

3. *Change of activity.* — Students should not be expected to listen intently for too long a time. Attempts to involve other senses should be made, such as providing visual stimuli or having students write for a few minutes.

The act of communication plays a vital role in the effective learning of students in the classroom. Teachers, by becoming aware of their strengths and weaknesses as communicators, can do a great deal to improve the sending and receiving of instructional and interpersonal messages in the classroom.

CHAPTER SUMMARY

The principles of instruction were addressed in this chapter, along with the strategic planning of lessons and instructional units. When learning principles and strategic planning are used in tandem, they increase the effectiveness and overall quality of planned instruction. The issue of classroom management was presented through highlighting three contrasting models of classroom discipline. Additionally, the art of communication applied to the lecture mode of teaching was discussed, with remedies for potential communication breakdowns in the classroom. When techniques for effective classroom management and communication are judiciously implemented by the teacher, the interactive process of teaching and learning is dramatically improved.

References

Canter, L., & Canter, M. *Assertive discipline: A take-charge approach for today's educator.* Santa Monica, Calif.: Canter & Associates.

Hunter, M. *Mastery Teaching.* El Segundo, Calif.: TIP Publications, 1982.

Wadsworth, B. *Piaget's theory of cognitive and affective development.* New York: Longman, Inc., 1984.

CHAPTER THREE

EVALUATION

Having discussed the development of curriculum and the implementation of instructional sequences to promote classroom learning, we turn now to the evaluation of these instructional and curricular-based decisions. The primary function of evaluation in the classroom is to determine the outcomes of the instructional sequence. These outcomes are directly related to the mastery of the target objectives but also include any relevant elements of planning the sequence (e.g., preassessing learners; forming appropriate objectives) and executing it (e.g, applying knowledge of learning principles; employing effective classroom-management strategies). Any factors which either positively or negatively influence the outcome of instruction, that is, which hinder or enhance mastery of the instructional objectives, are integral considerations in the evaluation process.

DEFINITION

We will discuss evaluation within the context of the following definition: the act of determining the degree to which an individual or group possesses a certain attribute. This might mean that the teacher determines that student X can correctly spell 85 percent of the third-grade spelling words, that one half of class K can identify three causes of World War I, or that student Q can go five minutes without exhibiting disruptive behavior.

The evaluation process is generally *student centered*. It involves looking at the outcomes of student learning and attempting to determine how to enhance their learning. While evaluation will include the role of the teacher, the specific instructional strategies and curriculum materials used, and the learning principles applied to instruction, the focus is still on how and why the students come out of the instructional sequence with what they do. The goal is to use evaluation to improve the instruction and thus ensure mastery of the intended objectives in class.

APPROACHES TO EVALUATION

Formal and *informal* evaluation are two approaches to day-to-day classroom evaluation. As the name implies, formal evaluation is done in a specific situation for a clearly stated purpose. It may be a state-mandated test administered to students, a collected set of drawings done by students, or a monthly checklist of student behaviors observed during physical education. What makes it formal is the predetermined intention behind collecting the data and the prescribed use which will be made of the information.

Information evaluation refers to those on-going forms of evaluation and unstructured attempts which teachers are continuously undertaking to gather relevant information regarding the progress of students. It may involve observing small-group sessions to determine the effectiveness of a grouping strategy or using a new system for distributing art supplies; whatever the teacher does on a spontaneous and informal basis to assess how things are going in the classroom is considered to be in the category of informal evaluation.

Both types have their place in the classroom. The teacher should be keenly aware of which type of evaluation is warranted in a specific situation. For example, formal evaluation procedures would be followed when determining a student's grade for a specific class. Informal evaluation procedures would be appropriate when deciding how best to use flash cards with the bilingual learners in a reading group. Teachers need to become adroit at employing both forms of evaluation effectively and prudently.

Another way in which evaluation is conceptionalized and applied to instruction is in terms of its timing and purpose. *Formative* and *summative* evaluation are two types of evaluation, differentiated by their placement and intent in regard to a given instructional sequence.

Formative evaluation is done during instruction, when the actual lesson, unit, or course is in a state of potential flux. When teachers gather on-going feedback regarding the effectiveness of the sequence (i.e., appropriateness of materials, quality of teaching style, interest level of students, etc.) to strengthen and possibly change it, they are employing formative evaluation. Teachers may do this spontaneously and often intuitively during instruction; sometimes they may embark on the instructional sequence with a preplanned set of formative evaluation questions to monitor the relative success of the sequence. Teachers may analyze the sequence at its conclusion; if the sequence is to be administered at another time, this analysis would be classified as formative evaluation. Effective, responsive instruction is promoted through such on-going scrutiny and through this internalized process of modification and improvement.

Summative evaluation, on the other hand, refers to evaluation done on an instructional sequence at the end of instruction. It may be done to assess specified aspects of a given curriculum which has been administered. It may be used to compare the relative effectiveness of two given sequences which are directed toward the same instructional end. The purpose here is not immediately to change or improve the sequence but simply to assess it, perhaps subsequently to eliminate, keep, or change the sequence. Summative evaluation *sums* up relevant data regarding the sequence for a *given* evaluative purpose.

EVALUATING TEACHING OUTCOMES

Evaluation often brings to mind test-taking activities or the assessment of paper-and-pencil products of students. While these constitute an aspect of evaluation, they are actually only a part of the total picture.

A distinction which may be helpful here is to look at two types of outcomes of the instructional sequence which are used in evaluation. These are *learner products* and *learner behaviors.*

Learner products are objects generated by students. Typically, they may be collected and evaluated to determine the level of performance demonstrated by students in the completion of the product. One may evaluate the effectiveness of the given sequence and determine the relative mastery of the target objective through an evaluation of each learner's product. The following list provides examples of the types of learner products found in the classroom: (1) an original short story, (2) an art project, (3) a math worksheet, (4) a written summary of a social studies film, and (5) a science report.

Although not an extensive list, these learner products are representative of what teachers use to assess student achievement and to determine flaws or strengths in the instructional sequence. For example, if the math worksheet is done successfully by the majority of the class, the teacher can assume that mastery of the underlying objectives has been furthered for most students; if the science reports consistently lack important requirements, then the teacher must look at the difficulty of the related objectives and at other factors, such as directions given, amount of time allocated for the report, and availability of resources necessary for completion of the report.

The second type of outcome of the instructional sequence is reflected in observable student behavior, where there is no tangible product. When used to evaluate student achievement, these behaviors must be systematically observed and recorded. The following list illustrates the kinds of learner behaviors which may be used in evaluation: (1) sharing materials in a learning center, (2) giving an oral presentation, (3) playing scales on a musical instrument, (4) participating in a simulation activity, and (5) reading a book during silent reading time.

This list represents the types of behaviors teachers observe and record to provide information on progress toward or mastery of a given objective. In addition, like learner products, learner behaviors provide specific information regarding the help or hindrance in the instructional sequence which affect student progress. Again, the cause is not always immediately clear but may be found in a variety of potential influencing factors.

Another important distinction in classroom evaluation is that made between *evaluation* and *measurement*. Measurement involves gathering descriptive data (of learner products and/or learner behavior) and relating this data to a standard of achievement, or norm. Evaluation refers to measurement techniques, in addition to more informal assessments of student progress; the emphasis here is always on results of the overall instructional process, including the sequence (planning, delivery, follow-up) and the observed change in student behavior (cognitive, psychomotor, and/or affective).

Application of measurement techniques for classroom use is focused mainly on two types: *norm-referenced* and *criterion-referenced* measurements. Norm-referenced measurement yields a comparative view of achievement, where student achievement is measured against group (normative) achievement. The Graduate Record Exam is an example of a norm-referenced measurement; selectivity is the goal of such measurement, where only a certain number of students, for example, may attain a certain score or may gain admittance to a specific program. When teachers employ a bell-shaped curve on a test, which designates a set number of certain grades which will be given, this is also a form of norm-referenced measurement; student achievement is compared to and affected by the achievement of others.

Criterion-referenced measurement is more in line with a view of evaluation as determining the possession of a certain attribute relative to a predetermined level of performance. In formulating objectives, one's goal usually will be to promote and then assess attainment of such a level of performance. Criterion-referenced (referring to the stated criterion or objective) measurement compares the learner to a predetermined standard of behavior. The relative effectiveness of instruction in achieving desired educational outcomes is determined through criterion-referenced measurement.

An example of this type of measurement would be a teacher-made test containing test items directly related to the objectives underlying instruction; the purpose of administering this instrument would be to determine the performance level of each student relative to these instructional objectives. Most teachers who use such forms of criterion-referenced measurement also advocate mastery learning, whereby assessment of student achievement is done holistically, over the length of the instructional sequence. Because mastery of the target objective is the primary basis for this type of evaluation, student work is often weighted more heavily toward the end of the instructional sequence, when students have been given ample practice time and feedback for achieving the given objectives. For example, for an English unit focused on acquiring essay writing skills, it would be appropriate to determine student mastery toward the end of the unit, when students are able to synthesize all learned elements to produce an essay. Therefore, grading would be based more on the cumulative effect of the instruction rather than being equally weighted throughout the unit.

Very often teachers use ready-made criterion-referenced tests which are included with basal programs or subject-matter textbooks. While these tests may be appropriate and are certainly time-saving, one must carefully check test items to make sure they match the objectives underlying the instructional sequences the students experienced. This is fair to students and also yields a more accurate assessment of the outcomes of instruction. Therefore, if certain items are not congruent with target objectives, they should be replaced with teacher-generated items more closely aligned with the objectives of instruction. Additionally, some premade tests may not call for higher-level thinking skills; for this reason, the teacher may wish to add short-answer questions or an essay question to round out the evaluation.

Often teachers will need to generate a test from scratch. In creating criterion-referenced teacher-made tests, one should be familiar with many important guidelines. Primary among these are the validity of the instrument and its reliability. Validity refers to the existence of congruence between the test items and the objectives; in other words, does it test what it means to test. Reliability means the consistency of the instrument in measuring achievement; in other words, would the results of the test be the same over time and in other situations (if no other changes were made in instruction, etc.).

There are two general categories of test-item formats typically used. One is the *selected response,* in which students choose a provided answer or response. Examples are (1) true-false, (2) matching, and (3) multiple-choice. The other is the *constructed response,* in which students generate an answer or answers to a posed question or complete a provided statement. Examples are (1) completion/fill-in-the-blank, (2) short-answer, and (3) essay.

Usually, it is helpful to students and useful in obtaining accurate feedback to include as many types of these test items as possible on a given test. Basic guidelines in the construction of such test items are explicated next.

True-false items should meet the following criteria: (1) be stated directly and be either clearly right or clearly wrong; (2) embody only one idea; (3) be placed randomly in terms of true and false statements; a slightly higher number of false should be provided; (4) be stated in positive form whenever possible; and (5) exclude absolutes, for example, "always" and "never."

In constructing matching-item tests, the teacher optimally would include two to three sets of matching items with six to eight items in each set. Also, each entire set of matching items should be included on a single page. Matching items in the left column are usually called premises, and those on the right are called responses. Matching items should adhere to the following guidelines: (1) contain premises which are longer than responses and (2) have responses that are greater in number than premises.

Multiple-choice items should meet the following criteria: (1) offer from two to five response choices (*note:* the introduction of the answer to be completed is called the *stem;* there is one correct answer; the rest of the choices are called *distractors*); (2) have a clearly stated stem which includes any material common to all distractors, to decrease reading time; (3) contain response choices of approximately equal length; and (4) contain attractive distractors but only one best answer.

Completion items, or fill-in-the-blank items, should meet the following criteria: (1) be stated to elicit only one brief answer; (2) leave only key words blank; (3) contain blank spaces of uniform length for each completion item; (4) avoid providing grammatical clues, for example, ''an'' or ''a''; and (5) provide the blanks, in most cases, at the end of the statement.

Short-answer items should meet the following criteria: (1) provide a clearly stated question containing adequate information needed to generate the response and (2) call for higher levels of thinking.

Essay items should meet the following criteria: (1) be stated clearly, setting limits on the range of possible responses; and (2) focus on a particular aspect of a given topic to avoid overwhelming the student.

As mentioned, there are approaches and measures other than tests which may be used in conducting evaluation in the classroom. Some of these include (1) interviews with students; (2) observations of student behavior using a predetermined checklist or form to increase accuracy of data collection; (3) records of student progress, such as cumulative records and anecdotal records; and (4) questionnaires which call for either free responses or forced-choice responses. Use of such measures increases the scope and range of the profiles of student progress.

GRADING

An inevitable and time-consuming aspect of evaluation called for in most school settings involves assigning grades to students. This may be disconcerting and even harrowing because many teachers enter the profession for the aesthetic experiences and opportunities for creative exchanges offered. However, the role of the teacher is that of both instructor and judge, and it is vital that the teacher deal with the duality of this role.

We contend that assigning a grade is a means of communicating something about the student's output to the student; it is not a subjective opinion of the perceived worth or potential of the learner. There are many dangers inherent in the whole process of grading which could directly affect students' self-images and attitudes toward learning.

A very careful explanation is needed when using and assigning grades in the classroom. Too often we hear, "I got an 'A' from Mrs. Little," revealing the fact that the student identifies the teacher as the source of the grade and not the product or work which has been completed. Students should realize that their *work* has been evaluated, not them. If students equate their feelings of self-worth with the grades they earn, there may be problems in later learning and life. We all know people who are in adulthood and are still seeking "As" and those who believe themselves to be "D" students in life.

We believe that the application of mastery learning in the classroom is an effective context in which to view and assign grades. If the teacher focuses on having students meet specific, predetermined goals and objectives, the process of grading will be more objective and based on observable student mastery of intended objectives. In this vein, students should be given repeated opportunities to master the objectives, being provided with guidance and additional instruction as needed.

Additionally, we believe it is damaging to students to put grades in a competitive context. If students are less capable than others, for example, in a given subject area, it is not beneficial to them to be compared with more capable peers. Posting grades on spelling tests, for example, may be pleasing to those who earn 100 percent on each test but may demoralize the learner who achieves only 50 percent each week despite sincere studying and effort.

Grades are perhaps the most powerful form of extrinsic motivation, and for that reason should be used judiciously by teachers. Students who perceive grades as having some inherent worth are missing the essence and purpose of learning. Teachers who hold up grades as the goal of an instructional sequence or a specific class are reinforcing this concept, albeit unwittingly.

Therefore, we advocate that grades reflect the meeting of specific instructional standards. We have an obligation to our students to assign them grades which truly reflect their degree of attainment of the objectives for which they are held responsible. To give students a higher grade because of the effort expended or their helpful, willing nature is both unprofessional and unfair. There is the typical dilemma of the low-achieving student who works very hard to improve; perhaps this student's output is greater than that of anyone else in the class, but the student still meets only 75 percent of the required standard. We believe that the teacher is obligated both to the student and to the student's next teacher to have the grade be an honest representation of the student's work. However, the student can and should be praised in a variety of ways and be made aware of the appreciation and awareness you have of the effort expended. One effective means of recording that effort is by the teacher entering appropriate information directly into the students' cumulative transcript so that the students' intrinsic levels of effort are recorded along with their objectively graded accomplishments.

In sum, the evaluation of students is a central aspect of the instructional process. It is at this stage that one determines if the desired instructional outcomes have been promoted and achieved through the instructional sequence.

CHAPTER SUMMARY

The evaluation of instruction was discussed in this chapter as a primarily student-centered vehicle for determining students' level of mastery of stated objectives. Several types of evaluation, applied depending upon the underlying instructional purpose, were included in the discussion: formal and informal, summative and formative. The distinction was made between evaluation and measurement, with a close look given to criterion-referenced measurement. Criteria for sound teacher-made tests were provided along with a philosophical discussion of assigning grades.

PART TWO

EXPANDING YOUR REPERTOIRE OF STRATEGIES FOR TEACHING AND ASSESSMENT

CHAPTER FOUR

MODULAR LEARNING CENTERS

Many educators view learning centers as classroom stations which contain only recreational materials, such as free-reading books, extra-credit puzzles, or games. In addition, learning centers are frequently perceived by educators to be appropriate only for elementary classrooms. We would like to expand this view and application of the use of learning centers to embrace more far-reaching instructional purposes than recreation and to increase its scope to include the secondary as well as elementary school levels.

In this chapter, the concept of the *modular learning center* will be discussed in terms of (1) the five ways in which modular learning centers may vary, (2) the principles for classroom use, (3) the six steps in creating a modular learning center, and (4) a checklist for assessing successful design and implementation of the center.

TYPES OF MODULAR LEARNING CENTERS

A classroom modular learning center can be described as a vehicle for providing a self-contained, self-directed learning experience in which pupils interact with materials and get immediate feedback about their learning. Modular learning centers vary in the following five ways:

1. *Subject area:* Language, reading, math, science, social studies, etc.
2. *Purpose:* A motivation center attempts to *stimulate the student's interest* in a particular subject, concept, or procedure. A concept center is designed to *impart knowledge*

about a concept, an idea, or a principle. A process center is designed to *teach the student how a particular object or process works,* for example, an experiment in chemistry or the game Four Square. It includes detailed step-by-step instruction.

3. *Time:* Some centers last for a day or two, while others might last for a few weeks or even a month.

4. *Length of task:* A center may be set up with a task that takes 10 minutes to complete or activities that take up to 30 or 40 minutes. Since attention spans increase as children get older, one would hope to find tasks of shorter duration in the primary grades and longer duration in the intermediate and upper grades.

5. *Number of students involved:* A center may be set up for individual students to interact with materials in the learning process or for small groups of students to work together.

PRINCIPLES FOR CLASSROOM USE

Effective use of the modular learning center is based on three underlying principles: (1) teacher independent, (2) intrinsically motivating, and (3) continuous feedback. The first principle states that the center must be *teacher independent.* This means that each student must be totally capable of using the center without the teacher's help. To ensure teacher independence, a modular learning center must have the following characteristics:

Directions
- directions for use of the center are posted in an obvious place
- directions are written or printed clearly and at the reading level of the student
- directions are stated in sequential order

Materials/ Equipment
- materials and equipment used in the center are pretested for snags or difficulties
- materials and equipment are suitable for student use and/or operation

Products
- samples of products that result from use of the center, for example, woven mats, score cards, or demand surveys, are displayed in the center
- students are told where to put their individual products from the center, for example, "Hang your poster on the bulletin board near the door." "Put the self-corrected results of your test in the red box to your left."

> • instructions for maintaining the center are posted in an obvious place
>
> *Materials*   • instructions include directions for returning materials
> • instructions describe what materials must be cleaned or replaced for the next user
> • instructions for maintenance can be used by the students as a checklist

Another way to make sure that centers are teacher independent is through the use of contracts. Some students find it difficult to make decisions about learning and then stick to those decisions. In such cases, it is helpful for the teacher and student to negotiate a formal agreement stating that the student will work on some center activity for a given length of time. This added structure and personal responsibility can often help a student develop independent work habits.

In summary, learning centers that are teacher independent include:

1. directions for use
2. pretested materials and equipment
3. display of center product
4. information about what is to be done with the student's center product
5. instructions for maintenance of the center

A second principle of learning centers is that the center should be *intrinsically motivating*. This means that the teacher has taken into account the interests and needs of the students so that the use of the center is desirable for the students. There are several ways of ensuring intrinsic motivation:

1. Students should be involved in the development of the concept of the center and the materials used.
2. Centers should develop out of the interests and needs of the specific students who will be using the center.
3. Centers should be designed to utilize materials *other than* paper and pencils, worksheets, and textbooks. The students will be more interested in items not usually found in school, such as puzzles, games, automatic feedback devices, pictures, films, filmstrips, and materials with which they can interact.
4. Centers should remain in operation only so long as students are interested in them and replaced when interest lags.
5. Centers should be colorful, attractive, well organized, and well maintained. They should provide privacy for one to three people and contain materials not easily broken or destroyed.

A third principle of learning centers is *continuous feedback.* Continuous feedback applies to the student primarily and to the teacher secondarily. To provide continuous feedback to the *student,* the learning center should give the students immediate knowledge of how well they are learning the skills and concepts associated with the center. Immediate feedback devices that the teacher could make include answer cards or sheets, flash cards with answers on the back, cassette tapes with prerecorded answers, factual bingo games and puzzles. Immediate feedback devices that are commercially produced include simulation games, electrical fact games, punch score sheets with key cards, and a number of other commercially prepared educational games that are pedagogically sound when properly developed through modular learning centers.

To provide feedback to the *teacher,* the learning center should provide opportunities for the students to indicate their particular response to the learning center experience. A sample questionnaire to elicit such a response follows:

_____ I enjoyed it a lot.

_____ I enjoyed it somewhat.

_____ I enjoyed it a little.

_____ I did not enjoy it.

Note: This questionnaire may be more detailed for secondary students. *Example at the primary level.*   At the early elementary level, it may be useful to provide students with a pictorial evaluation form to elicit feedback on satisfaction with the learning center. For example:

Circle one of these faces to tell how you feel about the learning center.

To provide feedback concerning learning centers in general, the student could periodically answer open-ended questions such as these:

- Which center did you like the most? Why?
- Which center did you like the least? Why?
- Do you have any ideas for centers that you would like to have in the classroom?
- In what ways did you benefit from using the centers?

The *teacher* receives continuous feedback about student learning in a variety of ways. In concept centers especially, a teacher-corrected evaluation instrument can be built into the center to check student progress. This instrument would be in addition to any self-corrected feedback devices that might be included for the student's own use. It should always be made clear to the student whether the center product will be self-corrected or teacher-corrected. In motivation centers, use of the center itself and requests for further experiences in the subject matter field are feedback to the teacher about student needs or readiness for the next step in learning.

In the process center, the product of the center is feedback to the teacher. For example: the student can now operate a filmstrip projector; can construct a three-dimensional cube; demonstrates a knowledge of game rules at recess time.

The teacher will probably want feedback on how frequently each center is being used. A form may be kept at the learning center so that students can make a record of their visits. Colored squares on a class chart could be used for the same purpose. As part of their contract, students who have difficulty making decisions should keep an individual chart in addition to making a group chart.

CREATING A MODULAR LEARNING CENTER

In developing a modular learning center there are six basic steps to follow.

Step 1: Decide whether you will develop a motivation center, a concept center, or a process center.

The purpose of a motivation center is to get students interested in a particular subject or concept. It attempts to give the student some inner reason, cause, incentive, or inducement for learning or studying about a given subject. For example, children in your fifth-grade class might have a negative attitude toward math. You could attempt to stimulate their interest by having a motivation center in which animals are kept. The center would be designed to demonstrate interesting applications of math, such as figuring how much food to buy each week to feed the animals (multiplication and division) or comparing the weight of each animal on the basis of food intake (functions, graphs, inequalities). Motivation centers nurture the students' interest in a subject by giving them positive experiences associated with the subject.

Example at the primary level. At the primary level, a motivation center may be designed to promote the skills of learning to write one's home address and to address an envelope. Thus, a large, colorful mailbox with a working chute for mail deposits might be placed in the center, along with materials to use in designing stamps. In this way, young children's excitement in using interesting manipulatives and in completing open-ended art projects would be tapped to further the underlying instructional objectives.

An example of a motivation center at the secondary level would be a grammar center using popular sports cars as the theme. A variety of assignments, changed regularly, would be provided for reinforcement and appropriate practice of grammatical concepts presented in class. Students might create parts-of-speech charts using a favorite car as the chart topic; writing a gramatically correct business letter to a car company for price and warranty information could be assigned. Thus, through the use of such a motivation center, interest in cars could provide a "vehicle" for motivating secondary-level students.

The concept center is usually the most cognitively oriented of the three types. It is designed to impart knowledge about a concept, an idea, or a principle. For example, in elementary social studies or high school economics, you may want to teach the concept of scarcity, limited resources versus unlimited wants. Your activities and materials would be designed and sequenced to give information about this concept. You would develop evaluation instruments and a check-list to determine the extent to which the concept had been learned. If your concept center were a music center, you may want students to learn the concept of harmony; in math, the center may be designed to teach the fundamental concepts of set theory; in science, the concept may be that of force; in reading, the concept of syllables may be explored. The point is that this type of center would be cognitively oriented. Upon completing the activities in the center, students would be able to (1) define the concept and (2) use the concept at some level above the recall level of learning.

The process center is designed to teach students how some device or process works. How do you fly a kite? How do you use a scroll saw in wood shop? For example, you may decide to put on a drama festival in your classroom. You might wish to make puppets for the play. The directions and procedures for making these puppets could be presented in a process learning center. You could also use a process center to explain how to make papier-mâché background scenery for the festival. Process centers might also be designed to teach the rules of simulation games or sports in which students participate.

Let us assume that you have decided to generate a concept center in spelling, math, and history. Once the decision is made as to what kind of center to develop, the next question is to determine the content for that particular center. The following guidelines should prove useful to the teacher:

Guideline A.   The content is appropriate for the age and interest level of the student. Poor selection for elementary: one-hundred complicated long-division problems. Good selection for secondary: review of basic computational skills in math.

Guideline B.   The learning center is the most appropriate format for the given content, that is, the material requires repetition, drill, or interaction with materials. Poor selection for elementary: chapters of history books; long selections of readings about various historical events. Good selection for secondary: a bingo game based on historical facts; a short study guide which augments the history unit.

Guideline C. The content of the center acts as a catalytic agent for other types of related learnings. Poor selection for elementary and secondary: center for dressing up in historical costumes; center has mirrors and elaborate costumes but no content. Good selection for elementary and secondary: a match game with cards containing time periods and clothing styles to put on a game board and/or filmstrip of various period clothing.

Guideline D. The expected learning that results is worth the effort of setting up the center. Poor selection for elementary: an arbitrary choice of spelling words. Good selection for elementary: activities based on a list of the most frequently misspelled words used by the students.

Step 2: Develop learning center objectives.

Once you have decided what kind of center is needed and what is appropriate content, the next question is, What are the objectives of this center? The objectives should not be stated in terms of your goals but in terms of student performance. What will students be able to do after completing those tasks that they were not able to do before? Practical experience suggests keeping the number and complexity of objectives to a minimum. Nine or ten objectives would probably be too many. Try, instead, to think of one or two objectives and aim at having the student apply these at higher levels, as opposed to having them learn all concepts at the rote level.

Step 3: Decide what constraints exist with regard to the objectives.

After writing your objectives, you deal next with the question, What are my constraints in achieving these objectives? One constraint may be that of space. Perhaps your objective is to have the students learn some principle, but it would take up half the room to teach it. The expected learning to result might not be worth the space. Resourceful teachers have used walls, bookshelves, cartons, hanging boxes, window sills, outdoor tables, cabinets, and even the ceiling to increase available space for centers. Another constraint may be school rules that limit available materials. Some schools, for example, prohibit teachers from nailing things to the walls or ceiling. After thinking of the constraints you are working with, modify your objectives to fit the physical and psychological constraints that might exist in your classroom.

Step 4: Preassess student knowledge related to the objectives.

At this point you have stated your objectives and revised them in terms of existing constraints. The next step is to design assessment instruments that will tell you the extent to which students have already achieved the objectives. The entry level of students may vary considerably within a given class. In some learning centers, the idea may be completely new to the students. In this case, a very simple verbal response from students might serve as a pretest. For example, you may ask the students, "Do you like rockets?" "What makes them fly?" If the answer to your first question is a vigorous "Yes!" and if the students are unable to answer the second question, you need no further preassessment activities. Once you have decided whether a formally recorded pretest is necessary, and if so, what it is going to be, there should be an easy way for the student to take this test. It might be talking into a recorder; it might include being interviewed by another student; it might involve the use of a checklist. You may need to modify your objectives on the basis of the results of your preassessment. Sometimes, you may wish to give students a guaranteed success experience and include some objectives that your assessment has indicated they can already achieve.

Step 5: List activities related to the objectives and the materials necessary for these activities.

The next step is to write out the potential ways in which the objectives could be achieved. For example, you might have story starters provided or picture displays with related questions to be answered. You might have a record that explains a process. You might have a filmstrip that sparks the students' interest. A series of cartoons might explain a specific concept. Remember that whatever you choose must be teacher independent and must achieve the stated objectives. Try to involve the students in this phase. Their ideas are invaluable, and they may have access to useful materials.

Step 6: Plan an evaluation to determine how well the students achieve the objectives of the center.

The last thing to plan is an evaluation to determine how well the center has led to mastery of its stated/intended objectives. This evaluation should give immediate feedback to the student. It can range from having students check their answers against an answer key to having them turn a tape over and listen to the correct answers. The important thing is that the students have an idea of their standing in respect to the learning center objectives. Later you may be interested in noting how well the students did, so you may want them to record their scores in a designated place or leave their corrected answer cards in a box at the center.

Figure 4–1 is a checklist which may be used by the teacher to determine if the principles and basic steps in developing a modular learning center have been incorporated into the planning and implementation stages.

Figure 4-1.   CHECKLIST FOR ASSESSING A MODULAR LEARNING CENTER

Have you:

_____ 1. Determined the type of center to be developed (motivation, concept, or process)?

_____ 2. Included students' suggestions for developing the centers and considered their interests and needs?

_____ 3. Set up guidelines to determine appropriate content for the center, ensuring that the activities are grade-level appropriate and relate directly to the stated objectives?

_____ 4. Formulated clear and measurable instructional objectives for the center?

_____ 5. Compensated for any constraints you were faced with in setting up and implementing this center?

_____ 6. Provided for thorough and appropriate preassessment of the learner's knowledge and skills with regard to the instructional objectives planned?

_____ 7. Created a list of ways in which the instructional objectives may be met, offering variety to the students in terms of their learning styles?

_____ 8. Provided for evaluation methods to determine the successful mastery of the instructional objectives?

_____ 9. Elicited student responses to determine the perceived benefit from using the center?

_____ 10. Evaluated the success of the lesson(s) in response to the original purpose for which the center was developed?

GUIDELINES FOR CONSTRUCTING A MODULAR LEARNING CENTER

The construction of a sturdy and long-lasting modular learning center is relatively simple and inexpensive. After the initial investment of time in assembling the center and the outlay for materials, the basic center may be used and reused for years.

Pegboard is generally used in learning centers because displayed directions and worksheets may be attached with brads through the pegboard holes. Panels of four feet by two feet should be used (see Figure 4–2). Two pieces are needed for a two-way center; three pieces are needed for a three-way center (Figure 4–2). A two-way center and three-way center may be attached to create a table-long center (Figure 4–2). Two hinges will be needed for joining the sides together, along with the hardware for attaching the hinges. If a three-way center is built, hinges are needed for each set of sides.

Figure 4–2. CONSTRUCTING A LEARNING CENTER

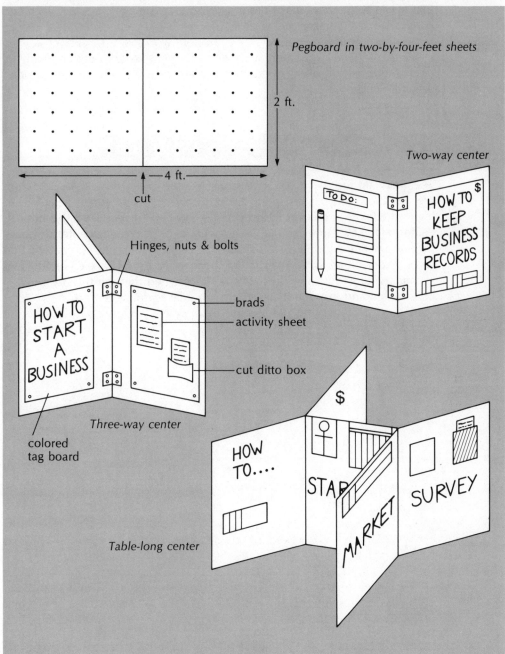

Pegboard in two-by-four-feet sheets

2 ft.

4 ft.

cut

Two-way center

TO DO:

HOW TO KEEP BUSINESS RECORDS $

Hinges, nuts & bolts

brads

activity sheet

cut ditto box

HOW TO START A BUSINESS

Three-way center

colored tag board

$

HOW TO....

START

MARKET

SURVEY

Table-long center

Contact paper may be used to cover the surface of the pegboard for aesthetic purposes. The edges may be covered with colored plastic tape. Often a large sheet of cardboard, a few inches smaller than the pegboard panel, is mounted on the surface, containing directions for the center, motivating pictures, or plastic sleeves to hold worksheets or answer keys.

Creativity and experimentation will lead the teacher to design highly attractive and useful modular learning centers for use in the elementary and secondary classroom.

CHAPTER SUMMARY

The rationale for the modular learning center and a discussion of its implementation were presented in this chapter, with three basic types highlighted: the motivational center, the concept center, and the process center. Five key variables and three essential principles for center development were outlined. Steps to follow for center design and implementation were given, along with a checklist for teacher use. The elementary and secondary classroom can be significantly enriched through the use of well-constructed and instructionally sound modular learning centers.

CHAPTER FIVE

EXPERIENCE-BASED TEACHING

Visualize students in two different classrooms working on the same behavioral objective in science. The students in both classes are seventh-graders. In classroom A, the students are reading a chapter on pulleys and are answering questions at the end of the book on the reading. The teacher has presented a ten-minute lecture preceding the assignment of the reading. In classroom B, the students are working in small groups. They have been given the following introduction by the teacher: "At a particular point in history, someone invented a device which proved useful to humankind. You have been given some pieces of metal and twine; I would like for you to try to invent the pulley. I have handed out a written description of what the pulley does from the glossary. I would like for you to try to make one in small groups and then discuss its potential value to people. When you are finished we will discuss your findings as a whole group."

In classroom A, the students are involved in a teacher-directed, traditional textbook activity to attempt to achieve the stated objective. In classroom B, the students are participants in a learning activity representative of *experience-based instruction,* whereby students pursue a behavioral objective through a direct, often hands-on experience. In this chapter, we will introduce experience-based education and its application to the elementary and secondary classroom.

WHAT IS EXPERIENCE-BASED TEACHING?

Experience-based instruction provides students with an alternative learning experience to the more widely used teacher-directed classroom approaches, such as the lecture method. This instructional strategy offers opportunities for active, personalized, and engaging learning activities for students of all ages. As the name implies, experience-based instruction gives students a setting or series of educational situations in the form of an involving initial experience orchestrated by the teacher. This base leads the student into a natural path of exploration and a hands-on investigation into a problem-solving situation or subject area.

The underlying educational goals of this strategy are (1) to increase the confidence and capability of the learner through active as opposed to passive participation in learning and (2) to create positive social interaction, thereby improving social relationships in the classroom.

This strategy is based theoretically on John Dewey's principle of "learning by doing." The assumption is that learners will get more out of the experience by active, personal involvement than they would get by simply looking on or by looking into the content or concept. Also, research has shown that students' problem-solving abilities are strengthened when the teacher assumes the noninterventionist role called for by this approach.

IMPLEMENTING EXPERIENCE-BASED
TEACHING TECHNIQUES

The procedures for setting up a "learn-by-doing" experience for students are as follows:

1. The teacher generates a carefully planned learning experience, which may be open-ended in its potential outcome or have a certain set of alternative outcomes.
2. The teacher may opt to present a challenging and motivating introduction to the experience.
3. Students may work individually but will more often work in small groups or as an entire group within experience-based learning.
4. Students are placed in real problem-solving situations, as opposed to vicarious situations. As an example, in small groups, students would be given pieces with which to build a miniature city as opposed to being told to imagine that they were going to create a miniature city of their own design.
5. Students actively participate in the established experience, making their own decisions and bearing the consequences of those decisions.
6. The entire class reassembles after the experience has run its course; to extend learning and understanding, the teacher leads a debriefing session based upon the varied experiences.

The debriefing has four parts, which are review, analysis, distillation, and integration.

1. *Review* the details of the event. If a specific student is involved, that student should verbally describe the occurrence from his or her vantage point.
2. *Analyze* the aspects of the event. In this step, the teacher should help the students identify the central problem or issue associated with the event.
3. *Distill* the principles and value premises related to the event.
4. *Integrate* the new information into the learning framework of the students. In this stage, the teacher relates the new information to the students' current knowledge base.

This last procedural step, that of debriefing the learning experience, that is, labeling and defining for the students what occurred and sharing findings, is the distinguishing characteristic of this instructional strategy, differentiating it from *experiential* learning. Experiential learning is primarily centered on providing students with open-ended, student-directed learning experiences which may or may not be put into a focused frame of reference or manageable context after the experience has transpired.

The Mini-Society Instructional System is a sound example of a thriving experience-based instructional program. The Mini-Society is a social studies and values-clarification program designed to increase economic literacy and decision making among young people; the program has been implemented in over one-hundred thousand classrooms and successfully incorporates the basic tenets of experience-based instruction. Students in grades three to six establish their own societies during forty-five-minute sessions, three times per week. They make the decisions regarding their society; the teacher is simply one equal member of the society. In addition, students bear the consequences of the decisions they make. The students participate in a teacher-led debriefing session after Mini-Society to clarify and put into a manageable context the students' learning experiences. For a more in-depth look at this program, see *Mini-Society: Experiencing Real-World Economics in the Elementary School Classroom* by Marilyn Kourilsky.

ROLE-PLAYING

Another application of experience-based instruction is *role-playing.* Generally most appropriate for ages nine and older, this strategy is extremely useful for dealing with social issues and for enhancing interpersonal communication in the classroom. In role-playing, again the teacher assumes a noninterventionist role in the classroom. The students take on the character, feelings, and ideas of another person in a specific situation.

There are numerous benefits to be derived from using this instructional approach in the classroom. First, when role-playing, children can act out and express feelings and opinions without risking sanctions or reprisals. They can also examine and discuss relatively personal and human issues without anxiety. Role-playing allows students to identify with real-world situations and with the ideas of others. Such identifications may pave the way for behavioral and attitudinal changes as students assume the character of another, that is, get into someone else's shoes. In this way, children are provided with a relatively safe and controlled setting in which to explore and demonstrate pervasive problems among groups or individuals.

In setting up a role-playing situation in the classroom, the teacher should follow the steps as outlined here:

Preparation and Instruction

1. The role-playing situation or dilemma is selected, generally by the teacher. The problem situations selected should be "sociodramas" which emphasize typical roles, problems, and situations familiar and important to the learners. The entire situation should be explained, including a description of the circumstances, individuals involved, and the basic positions taken by the characters.

The characters should not be based on actual individuals in the classroom; avoid stereotyping when designing characters, motives, etc. Be cautious that the role-playing situations do not in any way impinge upon the psychological privacy or security of the students.

2. Prior to the role-playing enactment, students should participate in warm-up exercises; these exercises are for all students, both active participants and active observers. Usually led by the teacher, these exercises are designed to relax the students, to help them get used to employing their imaginations, and to build group rapport and interaction. A variety of warm-up exercises may be used, such as charades, pantomiming, make-believe group actions like tossing a pillow across a room, everyone chewing four pieces of bubblegum, etc. Approximately five minutes is ample time for such exercises.

3. The teacher provides special instructions to the role-playing participants after presenting an overview of the situation to the entire class. The teacher may provide the background and basic characterizations in writing or through an oral explanation. It is usually best to select role-playing participants on a voluntary basis; a student should feel free to decline a role. In some cases, when students have actually observed a certain situation in real life, this may serve as a role-playing situation; the real-life participants may opt to reenact the experience. In briefing the actors for the role-play, the teacher should provide a detailed description of the personality, feelings, and basic beliefs of the characters; sometimes it is useful to build a past for the characters. In addition, the physical space and any props to be used in the role-play should be described.

4. The teacher provides roles and related instructions to all audience members. One effective way to provide students with an active part in the role-play is to set up two groups, each with a specific function to perform. Group 1 is comprised of *observers*. They are instructed to observe the following: (1) what individual characters are feeling, (2) what specific characters wanted out of the situation, and (3) why the characters responded the way they did. Group 2 is comprised of *speculators,* who attempt to view the role-play from a more objective, analytical viewpoint. It is their task to outline possible alternative courses of action which may have been undertaken by specific characters.

Dramatic Action and Discussion

5. The actors should proceed through the role-playing situation, while the audience participates in their preassigned roles.
6. The role-play should stop when the main points or behaviors have been observed.
7. The entire class then participates in a discussion centered on the role-playing situation. Each group in the audience should have the opportunity to present its observations or reactions. The participants themselves should be involved in the discussion. The discussion should be guided in such a way that the enacted role-play becomes directly applicable and meaningful to the lives of the students. The discussion should yield new insights into alternative ways of looking at and responding to a particular situation.

Evaluation of the Role-Play

8. Students should provide in writing or through an oral discussion the relative success or results of the role-play. Evaluative comments should be elicited about the meaningfulness of the role-play, the ways in which the situation could have been more effectively conceptualized, etc.
9. The teacher evaluates the perceived effectiveness and success of the role-play. Using notes taken during the role-play and the students' evaluative comments, the teacher determines any interpersonal, social, or academic growth which the role-play may have provided.
10. The teacher includes the performed and evaluated role-play in a journal or notebook for future use or for alteration.

The instructional strategy of experience-based learning has been covered in this chapter, with role-playing having been outlined for a representative look at such a strategy in action. What follows is a sample role-playing situation drawn from the classroom. It provides a real-life situation which may be enacted by teachers so that they can experience this instructional strategy. One student could play Mr. or Mrs. Franklin, and another could play Mr. or Ms. Jacobs. The setting could be a parent-teacher conference.

Role-Playing Case Study:
The Parent/Teacher Conference

Nancy Jacobs is a sixth-grade teacher. She has been teaching for seven years. Her class is considered by others on the staff to be well run and creative. However, this year she has a student, Becky Franklin, who is causing problems in the classroom. There are continuous disturbances at the table where Becky sits with five other students.

Becky does not turn in homework assignments, will not take part in the learning centers, and insists on bothering other students when they are at the learning centers. Ms. Jacobs, well known for her patience, tries to work with Becky—trying contracts, positive reinforcement, and a variety of other techniques which have worked for her over the years.

After several weeks of the problem not only continuing, but eventually worsening, Ms. Jacobs decides to call a parent conference. Ms. Jacobs begins discussing the situation which has developed.

Mrs. Franklin explains that Becky is the model child at home. She *offers* to do the dishes, clean out the bird cage, and any other chores which come up. She gets along beautifully with her brothers and never fights with them. She has a calm manner always when she is with the family. Mrs. Franklin suggests that the problem most likely lies with Ms. Jacobs. Because Becky has always adored school and all of her other teachers, Mrs. Franklin insists that it must be *this* teacher who isn't making an effort to reach Becky.

An exampe of a role-playing situation which may be used with students follows. A checklist, Figure 5–1, is also provided for the teacher when designing, implementing, and evaluating such an instructional strategy.

Role-Playing Case Study:
The Homecoming Dance

Denise and Jerry have known each other since the second grade and have become really close since they started junior high. As ninth-graders they spend all of their time between classes and at lunch together. About one month after school has started, Denise meets a new student at the school; he's from out of state. His name is Darryl. He comes from a wealthy family and considers himself a lady's man. He and Denise have three classes together, and she volunteers to show him around, introduce him to her friends, and help him get familiar with the school system. Jerry is hurt but keeps it to himself.

Darryl asks Denise to go to the Homecoming Dance. She is thrilled. On the night of the dance, she is waiting for Darryl to pick her up; he calls and says he is sick. Denise decides, after a lot of thinking, to call Jerry. He says he would love to take her, and comes over to pick her up. When they walk into the dance, Denise sees Darryl on the dance floor with another girl.

Figure 5-1. ROLE-PLAYING CHECKLIST

Have you:

_____ 1. Carefully planned an open-ended situation in which the characters can interact?

_____ 2. Incorporated the interests of the students into the role-playing dilemma?

_____ 3. Ensured that the students' privacy has not been invaded in the construction of the role-playing situation?

_____ 4. Explained the role-playing situation to the students?

_____ 5. Asked for *volunteers* to participate in the role-play?

_____ 6. Provided instructions for the participants in the role-play which give adequate information with which to work?

_____ 7. Provided warm-up exercises for the students prior to the enactment of the role-play?

_____ 8. Assigned the audience to the roles of observers and speculators and clarified their responsibilities?

_____ 9. Debriefed the role-play once it has been enacted?

_____ 10. Evaluated the success of the role-play using teacher feedback and student comments and input?

Figure 5–1 is a checklist that incorporates the principles that underlie role-playing and the steps necessary for successful implementation of the strategy.

CHAPTER SUMMARY

Experience-based instruction has been discussed in this chapter in terms of two of its most useful classroom applications: hands-on learning experiences and role-playing. Techniques for implementing an experience-based instructional sequence were outlined, including the debriefing session, which follows and clarifies the direct experience. Role-playing was discussed as an effective way to promote positive social interaction skills and interpersonal communication in the classroom. This strategy is highly effective and viable for enhancing and personalizing the learning environment in the classroom.

Reference

Kourilsky, M. *Mini-Society: Experiencing real-world economics in the elementary school classroom.* Menlo Park, Calif.: Addison-Wesley, 1983.

CHAPTER SIX

INQUIRY-BASED TEACHING

Inquiry-based teaching is a student-centered strategy whereby groups of students inquire into an issue or seek answers to posed content questions within a clearly outlined procedure and group structure. To present the reader with the range and versatility of this model, we will discuss a generalized approach to inquiry and two major strategies for classroom implementation. The generalized approach we call *problem-centered inquiry;* the related strategies are *discovery-oriented* and *policy-based inquiry.*

For each mode of inquiry, we will provide the underlying assumptions on which it is based, present the procedures and guidelines for classroom implementation, discuss the role of the teacher, and provide a classroom example to translate the model into practice. Also, we will include a brief discussion of cooperative learning, a philosophical and instructional approach which offers an interesting context within which to present inquiry opportunities to students.

As Figure 6–1 indicates, both subsets of problem-centered inquiry advocate the active pursuit of information and ideas, but with a different focus and desired outcome.

DISCOVERY-ORIENTED INQUIRY

Discovery-oriented inquiry refers to academic situations in which small groups of students (generally four to six members) pursue answers to posed or encountered inquiry topics. In such situations, a findable, knowable concept or piece of information is to be "discovered" by the students. (When this

Figure 6-1. PROBLEM-CENTERED INQUIRY

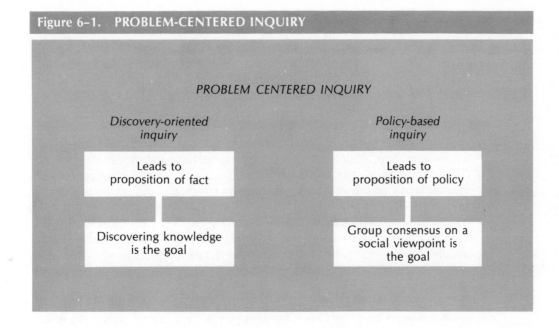

PROBLEM CENTERED INQUIRY

*Discovery-oriented
inquiry*

Leads to
proposition of fact

Discovering knowledge
is the goal

*Policy-based
inquiry*

Leads to
proposition of policy

Group consensus on a
social viewpoint is
the goal

model is applied to the entire class, as a part of inquiry activities, it is sometimes referred to as social inquiry. See *Models of Teaching* by Joyce and Weil for more information on this approach.)

The underlying assumptions on which this mode of inquiry are based are as follows: (1) critical thinking skills and deductive reasoning are enhanced when students collect evidence related to group-generated hypotheses; (2) students benefit from group experiences in which they communicate, share responsibilities, and jointly seek knowledge; (3) learning activities presented in a spirit of shared inquiry and discovery increase motivation and promote active participation.

Although most educators would agree that these goals are desirable and essential, few instructional strategies offer the framework within which to achieve such goals. The steps for implementing this mode of the inquiry-based model are explicated next.

In most cases, there is an initial situation in which an inquiry focus is presented to the students. As they inquire into the problem, they then follow the procedural steps outlined here:

1. Clearly identify and define the situation, that is, the inquiry focus.
2. Pose a question of fact.
3. Formulate a hypothesis (or hypotheses) to answer the question in step 2.

4. Collect information relevant to the hypothesis (or hypotheses) and test each hypothesis against the collected data.
5. Formulate an answer to the original question and state the answer as a proposition of fact. (The answer should represent a synthesis of the hypotheses proposed and the results of hypothesis testing and information gathering.)

This inquiry process calls for a teacher to be a facilitator, resource person, and group counselor. Typically, teachers present students with pieces of knowledge; here students are encouraged to seek the knowledge themselves. Therefore, the teacher must meet the following criteria for successful implementation of this instructional strategy: (1) clearly define inquiry topics which are appropriate for the learners, (2) establish groups which are balanced academically and socially, (3) clearly explain the task and provide feedback to groups in a responsive and timely manner, (4) intervene sparingly to ensure healthy interpersonal interaction and task progress, and (5) provide evaluation, in some form, to the group regarding both their group progress and the outcome achieved.

A classroom application of this instructional approach follows. As you read, consider the effect such an assignment could have on the students' sense of initiative, curiosity, and responsibility for their own learning.

Sixth-Grade Level

Group structure. Six groups of five students are used. Each group has (1) a group leader, (2) a scribe/recorder, (3) a prompter, (4) a discussion monitor, and (5) a summarizer. (*Note:* These roles are included here to indicate the types of potential roles available in inquiry-based groups. See Figure 6–2 for complete role descriptions and alternative group roles.)

Situation. Students are about to begin studying the early explorers of America and the fundamentals of early navigation. Students view a film on the sailing vessels used during the time of Columbus, highlighting navigational instruments.

Posed question. A simple compass is given to each group and the students are asked, "How does a compass work?" and "Why is a compass necessary?"

Formulate initial hypothesis. From available group knowledge and educated guesses, students form a tentative hypothesis on how they think the compass works and its intended purpose. The group leader may elicit ideas from each member to ensure optimum group participation. No outside resources may be used at this point.

Figure 6–2. SAMPLE INQUIRY GROUP ROLES

Group Leader	Generally initiates discussion and has primary responsibility for having group stay on task and complete assignments. Meets with the teacher formally to discuss group progress and needs. Disseminates information to the group from the teacher. Presents group information and ideas to the rest of the class or to other groups.
Scribe/Recorder	Depending on what recordkeeping and written work is required, the scribe is in charge of the group's written material. This may be kept with the group on an on-going basis or may be turned in. May also keep checklists of compiled work and attendance of group members.
Discussion Monitor	Ensures that the discussion is proceeding on track and that all points of view are acknowledged and incorporated into the discussion. Monitors the tone of the discussion to keep it open and supportive.
Prompter	Keeps track mentally or through the use of a group roster checklist of the participation of all group members. Encourages everyone to contribute and tries to draw out more detailed explanation from more reticent members.
Summarizer	Throughout the discussions and at the conclusion of each inquiry session, summarizes the key points raised and summarizes specific tasks completed and those still incomplete. Calls for questions from the group to clarify status of group progress and goals.
Devil's Advocate	Purposely interjects opposing points of view to test the strength and validity of presented arguments. Challenges speakers by offering counterarguments when possible.

Collect information and test hypothesis (hypotheses) against collected data.
From the agreed-upon hypotheses of the group, the students use subsequent inquiry sessions to collect information to support their hypotheses. They determine what information they need to find and the sources of such information. They may do such things as conduct library research, contact an expert in the field, take apart the compass, and try to make their own compass. Using such sources and gathered evidence, students will test out their initial hypotheses to see whether they are valid and complete.

Answer the original question. Students use the data collected and the results of their hypothesis testing to formulate answers to original questions. The students generate propositions of fact, which may be modifications of the original hypotheses, to address the posed inquiry questions. Generally, a complete record is presented, documenting the group process, including initial hypothesis formation, subsequent investigation and testing, and the ''discovery'' of propositions of fact. Examples of student-formed propositions of fact about the compass may be: (1) the compass needle will point north if no nearby metal objects attract it, (2) opposite poles of magnets attract and like poles repel, (3) the earth acts as if a large magnet were inside it, and (4) the needle of the compass is magnetized and lines up with the earth's north magnetic pole.

The mode of presenting such findings may take a variety of forms; the group spokesperson may give an oral summary, the group recorder may fill out a questionnaire on the group process and findings, or a discussion may be held to share phases of the conducted inquiries in arriving at the group findings. Usually, a questionnaire is given to all students to elicit their level of overall satisfaction with the group experiences. See Figure 6–3 for an example of an appropriate instrument to be administered at the conclusion of the inquiry process.

A variation of this example would be to have each group pursue a different inquiry focus instead of a single one. For example, instead of all groups investigating the compass, each group could study a different aspect of the time period. One group might investigate how early sailing vessels worked while another looked into reasons for high death rates on the voyages. Then students would share with the whole class their initial inquiry focus and the steps taken in pursuing answers.

As illustrated by this example, students in the discovery-oriented inquiry process take an active part in discovering knowledge and putting it into a meaningful context. By sharing ideas and collected information as a group, students expand their questioning strategies and increase their social interaction skills. Knowledge arrived upon in this way is somewhat akin to an earned trophy, a sort of personalized group victory, and sparks an on-going quest for discovered knowledge.

For inquiry topics, a primary source we have found to be fertile is one's own students. They can generate numerous questions for investigation based on their own areas of interest. Contests can be held for such topics, an inquiry suggestion box could be set up, or a weekly questionnaire entitled ''What Questions Have Come Your Way This Week?'' could be administered. (See Figure 6–4 for examples.)

This instructional strategy is applicable from early elementary to graduate-level study. The key is to determine the intellectual capabilities and social skills of one's students and plan the inquiry sessions accordingly. For example, for early elementary students a suitable topic may be, Why do the coats of certain mammals change color during the different seasons? while

Figure 6–3. EVALUATING DISCUSSION OF DISCOVERY-ORIENTED INQUIRY

Note: 1, 2, 3 represent positive responses, 1 being the most positive; 4 represents a neutral response; 5, 6, and 7 represents negative responses, 7 being the most negative.

Task Environment

1. Clear definition of the inquiry focus	1	2	3	4	5	6	7
2. Clearly stated factual questions	1	2	3	4	5	6	7
3. Objective analysis of each initial hypothesis by presentation of evidence	1	2	3	4	5	6	7
4. Objective analysis of each initial hypothesis by presentation of logic	1	2	3	4	5	6	7
5. Final hypothesis — reflection of the results of hypothesis testing and information gathering	1	2	3	4	5	6	7

Interpersonal Environment

1. Cooperative as opposed to competitive	1	2	3	4	5	6	7
2. Degree of permissiveness (freedom to speak one's mind)	1	2	3	4	5	6	7
3. Flexibility in adherence to rules and regulations	1	2	3	4	5	6	7
4. Effective leadership (each performs given task)	1	2	3	4	5	6	7
5. Optimum use of member resources	1	2	3	4	5	6	7

Comments:

graduate students may investigate, What instructional strategies are most appropriate for learning disabled students? The topic must spark genuine interest in the students, so that they will be able to sustain motivation over time; additionally, sources of information to test the formulated hypotheses must be available but not too simple to locate. The topic must warrant the time and effort expended and should promote intellectual curiosity and social interaction.

An additional source for inquiry topics is *Newton's Apple,* a public television series predicated on the inquiry-centered approach. Questions generated from the viewing audience are presented and answered during the segment. Showing students a segment of the show could be a useful way to introduce this instructional strategy and model the spirit of inquiry and discovery.

Figure 6–4.   SAMPLE STUDENT-GENERATED INQUIRY TOPICS

Elementary
1. How can fish live under water?
2. What makes an airplane fly?
3. How were the pyramids built?
4. Why don't we have a king and queen in the United States?
5. What do insects eat?
6. How do blind people read?

Secondary
1. Why is certain big-game hunting allowed and even encouraged?
2. What causes heart attacks?
3. How do babies learn/acquire language?
4. Why did the American Indians lose most of their land?
5. What are causes of teenage suicide?
6. How are economic resources allocated in the Soviet Union?

POLICY-BASED INQUIRY

Policy-based inquiry is a more proactive form of inquiry dealing with the establishment of propositions of policy, that is, a "what should be" (action-oriented) statement as opposed to a proposition of fact, a "what is" statement. This differs from discovery-oriented inquiry primarily by the nature of the inquiry and the intended goal; social issues and related policy are the focus and the goal is group consensus on the targeted policy. In a nation oriented toward discussing policy and resolving problems, it is appropriate and even essential that our students have a group experience whereby they identify and define social problems through recommended policy.

The primary purpose of this instructional strategy is to teach students how to be reflective about significant social problems. The underlying assumptions of the approach are that (1) a major goal of education should be the reflective examination of values and issues of current importance; (2) social science should be learned in the course of the attempt to develop solutions to significant problems; and (3) inquiry situations allow students to develop an awareness of and facility with group roles, functions, and decision-making techniques.

To implement this mode of inquiry, the groups follow specific steps. Keeping in mind that the emphasis here is on social issues, consider the myriad of benefits students could derive from participating in the inquiry process outlined here:

1. Establish inquiry groups. Have a wide range of intellectual and social skills represented in each.
2. Introduce inquiry topic(s) to the groups. They should produce genuine puzzlement and generate group interest.
3. Establish a tentative proposition of policy related to the topic, that is, a "should be" statement. It may include one or more proposed solutions to the initial problem.
4. Define all terms in the proposition of policy.
5. Explore the logical validity and the internal consistency of the proposition and its supporting contentions.
6. Collect evidence to support the contentions.
7. Analyze the proposed solutions and achieve a group position.
8. Evaluate the group process.

During this process, many sessions will involve group discussion of independently researched materials brought to the group. Individuals are responsible for finding specific pieces of evidence to support group contentions. This process is organized and monitored by the group itself. Essentially, steps five through six are the steps in which group progress depends on individually conducted outside research.

In addition to these steps, three components are essential for successful implementation of this mode of inquiry: (1) specific leadership functions must be executed within the group, (2) specialized roles for each group member must be assigned, and (3) an effective and appropriate emotional climate must be established and maintained. Therefore, in addition to understanding the purpose and procedure of the inquiry process, students must become familiar with and adept at incorporating these three components.

To proceed effectively through the steps of the inquiry process, students must know how to achieve the movement toward group decision-making. The following seven functions must be performed in each successful group. Such functions may be assigned to a group leader but ideally will be allocated to the entire group, providing each member with a specific role. With such assignment of specialized functions, students assume ownership for fulfilling them. The teacher may wish to role-model and signpost these functions in an introductory inquiry session and then have students discuss the importance of each one at the end of the session.

The functions within the successful inquiry group are as follows:

1. Make an outline of the inquiry focus, including proposed initial contentions and tentative propositions related to the topic.
2. Initiate the discussion.
3. Ensure active participation, drawing in more timid members, and balancing more controlling verbose members.
4. Keep the discussion on track.

5. Make occasional summaries of on-going discussions.
6. Keep the discussion from becoming one-sided.
7. Test the information stated and reasoning used.

These seven functions, then, would be divided among the group members, depending on the various strengths represented in the group. A strong group leader is usually needed to provide follow-through and support of all functions.

For the emotional climate of the groups, including optimum group comfort and effectiveness, certain conditions need to be present. The group process should be viewed and experienced as cooperative, not competitive. Students must feel free to express themselves openly. There must be flexibility in dealing with group situations. Effective leadership must be present. And, finally, member resources must be used effectively.

In conclusion, the groups involved in the inquiry need to follow the procedural steps of the inquiry and also need to gain facility in ensuring the execution of the leadership functions, group roles, and conditions of the emotional climate. Additionally, group members should have the opportunity to evaluate the group process on an on-going basis. For a sample form which provides an evaluation of the task environment and interpersonal environment, see Figure 6–5.

The role of the teacher during policy-based inquiry sessions is one of counselor, sharpener, and focuser. The teacher should be available to groups who express a need for assistance in their group interaction skills, a sharpening of their arguments and evidence collection, or a focusing of their discussions and evidence compilation. The teacher does not lead inquiry sessions, except perhaps in an introductory session, as previously discussed. The teacher often will circulate through groups to assess the progress and emotional climate of the sessions and provide feedback when necessary.

In selecting and generating policy-based inquiry topics for classroom use, keep in mind that such topics are essentially discussion topics, whereby alternative solutions may be proposed and investigated. This inquiry approach combines salient elements of discovery-oriented inquiry and the advocacy-based model; students seek to discover answers to stated questions and also compile evidence to support their viewpoints. However, in advocacy, two opposing viewpoints are juxtaposed and teams support or refute the proposition of policy. Here, stated policy problems allow for a more open-ended approach as students move toward resolution and group consensus.

Other important factors in topic selection are the students' age and maturity levels, social and political consciousness, and areas of high-level interest and concern to them.

The following are policy-based inquiry topics which have been used to generate successful and engaging inquiry experiences for students:

Figure 6–5. EVALUATING DISCUSSION OF POLICY-BASED INQUIRY

Note: 1, 2, 3 represent positive responses, 1 being the most positive; 4 represents a neutral response; 5, 6, 7 represent negative responses, 7 being the most negative.

Task Environment

1. Clear definition of problem	1	2	3	4	5	6	7
2. Logical and systematic investigation of the problem	1	2	3	4	5	6	7
3. Objective analysis of problem by presentation of evidence	1	2	3	4	5	6	7
4. Adequate diagnosis of problem — reasoning	1	2	3	4	5	6	7
5. Solution — availability of alternatives	1	2	3	4	5	6	7
6. Solution — degree of relatedness to previous findings	1	2	3	4	5	6	7
7. Solution — reflection of group's potential	1	2	3	4	5	6	7

Interpersonal Environment

1. Cooperative as opposed to competitive	1	2	3	4	5	6	7
2. Degree of permissiveness (freedom to speak one's mind)	1	2	3	4	5	6	7
3. Flexibility in adherence to rules and regulations	1	2	3	4	5	6	7
4. Effective leadership (each performs given task)	1	2	3	4	5	6	7
5. Optimum use of member resources	1	2	3	4	5	6	7

Comments:

1. What can be done in the United States to control the high rate of unwanted teenage pregnancy?
2. What can be done locally to lower youth-gang violence?
3. What should be the U.S. policy, if any, toward latch-key children?
4. What should be the U.S. policy toward gun control?
5. What should be the U.S. policy toward compulsory service in the armed forces?

As the reader can see, these topics allow for a range of viewpoints and potential solutions; they could capture the interest of most students, and they could lead to interesting discussion sessions and research efforts.

In translating this mode of inquiry to classroom practice, the following sample is provided:

Course	Tenth-grade English
Inquiry Topic	What policy should be established regarding leaving campus at lunchtime?
Inquiry Groups	Six groups of six students Sample group roles are (1) leader, (2) scribe, (3) prompter, (4) discussion monitor, (5) summarizer, and (6) devil's advocate
Introduction and Orientation	This issue has generated much interest and discussion schoolwide. Within the inquiry groups, students are assigned to pursue solutions to the problem and to generate a proposal for resolution. Each group discusses the topic and forms a tentative outline reflecting the group members' views.
Generation of Proposition(s) of Policy	Group determines possible solutions to be further investigated and discussed. For example, these could be: (1) seniors should be allowed to leave campus at noontime; (2) in addition, a weekly lottery should be held of underclasswomen or men who are on the honor roll; twenty students should be selected at random from the group.
Definition of Terms Exploration and Evidence Compilation	Group defines each important term in the proposition to ensure clarity and group consensus. Group members determine what facts and evidence are needed to support their proposed solutions. Responsibilities are divided among the group members: (1) Two students will conduct interviews with staff and students during lunch, (2) two students will research the policy on other local campuses and the results, and (3) two students will research data on effects on schooling, attendance, and attitudes when students are able to leave campus. Groups bring updates of progress and findings to each inquiry session.
Achieving a Group Position and Summarization	The findings of the group and the arguments which have been built are formed into generalizations about the topic. Key contentions, pieces of evidence, and social factors are summarized. Each group writes an

essay containing its initial propositions, proposed solutions, and a summary of the group viewpoint. Responsibilities for the written work are divided among group members.

Evaluation   The groups share their essays with the rest of the class, one member from each group reading the essay aloud. Each group receives a group grade for its essay. Each group member completes an evaluation form reflecting his or her satisfaction with the group process and the actual outcome. (See Figure 6–5 for sample form.)

This sample policy-based inquiry reflects a key element of this mode, namely, the movement toward group decision making related to the topic. There will be various points of view represented during the course of the inquiry, group consensus being the overriding influence. Through such an experience, students gain an understanding of the importance of dealing with important social issues and see the benefit of working together to reach an agreement about proposed solutions. Additionally, through on-going discussions and extensive investigation into the topic, the studied policy becomes more "alive" and relevant to the lives of the students.

Example at the primary level.   The previous example calls for a rather high level of critical thinking and group independence generally characteristic of secondary students. However, this approach may be scaled down for use with students from kindergarten to middle-school age. The key is to retain the essential elements of the model and to keep the inquiry focus within the direct experience of the students. For example, students may go through the main steps of this inquiry model in small groups, resolving such topics as (1) What can be done to make the school grounds more attractive? (2) What can be done about petty theft in the classroom? or (3) What can be done to make the classroom a safer place?

As the reader can see, these are more simplistic topics and are of immediate concern and relevance to the students. However, the same outcomes of the inquiry process are still promoted: analysis, proposing alternatives, group discussion and consensus, and generating an end product or proposal.

In sum, problem-centered inquiry, as opposed to other forms of inquiry in the classroom, places an emphasis on the product; this product may be a discovered piece of knowledge or a decision reached by the group. The relative success of the group process in such settings is analyzed and assessed in terms of whether it contributed to or detracted from the end product. The group process itself serves as the vehicle for solving a particular problem. Through such group experiences, students see first-hand the value of accountability, the positive interaction, the clearly defined goals and responsibilities, and the importance of achieving group goals.

COOPERATIVE LEARNING

The inquiry approaches which have been presented here may be enhanced by incorporating them into an educational framework called *cooperative learning.* Collaboration and cooperation within groups is advocated through the cooperative learning model. (See *Circles of Learning* by David Johnson, et al. for a full discussion of cooperative learning.)

Through this model, positive peer interaction and the achievement of mutual goals are promoted through small-group activities which dovetail very well with such outlined group goals and structures. Implementing these educational strands simultaneously would serve to promote the social interaction and group skills of students as well as their intellectual development.

The benefits of providing students with inquiry-based instruction in small-group settings are extensive and potentially long lasting. The student, as an eventual member of society's electorate, experiences the importance and rewards of effective group interaction and group consensus. The spirit of discovery and investigation brought about through such educational opportunities is something which can infuse the classroom with increased motivation and student autonomy.

CHAPTER SUMMARY

This chapter has discussed the rationale for and implementation of the efficacious instructional strategy of inquiry-based teaching. We presented the two related strategies of policy-based inquiry and discovery-oriented inquiry, conceptualized here as problem-centered inquiry. Critical thinking skills, group cooperation, and motivation are promoted through the successful application of this model in the elementary and secondary classroom. It calls for a shift in the teacher role and for careful planning in topic selection and group formation; such effort yields definite benefits for students who actively seek knowledge and challenge one another as they do so.

References

Johnson, D., Johnson, R., Holubec, E. J., & Ray, P. *Circles of Learning.* Alexandria, Va.: Associates for Supervision and Curriculum Development, 1984.

Joyce, B., & Weil, M. *Models of Teaching.* Englewood Cliffs, N.J.: Prentice-Hall, 1980.

CHAPTER SEVEN

STUDENT-CENTERED
ADVOCACY LEARNING

Often referred to as the process of debate, *advocacy learning* offers an alternative approach to didactic instruction in the classroom that gives students the opportunity to examine issues of social and personal significance through direct involvement and personal participation. Advocacy learning calls for students to focus on a predetermined topic and defend a point of view related to that topic. In this chapter, an overview of advocacy learning will be provided including the basic principles underlying its use and the steps for implementing the model.

WHAT IS AN ADVOCACY MODEL
OF INSTRUCTION?

Advocacy learning lets learners become advocates of a particular point of view related to an established topic. Students use research skills, analytical skills, and speaking and listening skills as they participate in such classroom advocacy experiences; they are faced with controversial issues and must develop a case to defend their point of view within a set of specific guidelines and objectives.

In advocacy learning, students participate in a debate with two teams of two students each. Usually, each team will debate on a topic different from those of the other class members. Therefore, in a class of thirty-two students there would be eight debate topics. In some cases, the teacher may decide that one debate in the classroom is most appropriate; for example, in a fifth-grade classroom, the teacher may decide that the students need exposure to the process of debate and will select four students to present a debate to the class. Ideally, the topic directly relates to the needs or interests of the students; perhaps the topic of longer recesses is of primary interest to the students. Like any instructional strategy, its use will be modified by the teacher to meet the specific needs of the particular group of students.

PRINCIPLES OF ADVOCACY LEARNING

Advocacy learning is based on several sound principles of learning. First, when students are directly involved in researching and presenting a debate, they have more ego wrapped up in the process than they would in a traditional lecture situation. Also, student interest and motivation are generally increased because of the nature of the debate process; students focus on an issue of concern to them and sometimes to society at large. An example of a debate topic might be the school dress code or the need for an after-school sports program in which the students are highly interested. They may debate on social issues of personal concern such as child abuse or teenage pregnancy. In addition, students in general will learn more about their topic and the other topics presented in class if they have been directly involved in the experience of debate; student retention of the basic components of an issue and principles of effective argumentation have been shown to be significantly strengthened through such a process.

Advocacy learning is applicable to both elementary and secondary learning. Depending on the level of the students, the model can be expanded or condensed.

The instructional approach of advocacy learning has been shown to develop students' skills in logic, problem solving, critical thinking, oral communication, and written communication. Affective gains, such as an enhancement in self-concept and a sense of autonomy, may result from such learning opportunities. When students find an effective vehicle by which to explore and argue on a variety of meaningful topics, they are able to expand their repertoire for effective interpersonal communication. They gain confidence in their ability to present their point of view and critically analyze the contentions and ideas raised by another in the debate.

HOW TO IMPLEMENT
ADVOCACY-BASED LEARNING

The basic steps in setting up a debate are outlined here:

1. Select an appropriate debate topic, considering the level of the students and the relevance of the topic to the curriculum and interests of the students.

2. Select two debate teams, two students per team for each topic.
3. Explain the function of each team to the class.
4. Provide guidelines and assistance for students to help them prepare for the debate.
5. Hold the debate. Provide the audience with specific observational functions to perform during the debate.
6. Hold class discussion/debriefing after the debate.

Given these initial steps, it is important to discuss further the basic principles of debate and provide a set of terms and definitions for advocacy learning. As stated, advocacy, or debate, is an oral controversy in which students take opposing sides on a stated proposition of policy. A proposition of policy addresses "what should be," stating that a particular policy be initiated (e.g., the United States should have a balanced budget). All of the propositions students debate are *propositions of policy*. These policy propositions call for a change from the status quo, the present system, and recommend that a new policy be implemented. Examples of policy propositions appropriate for the elementary level would be:

1. Sixth-graders should be allowed to go to dances at the junior high
2. Students should be able to vote at school-wide assemblies
3. Computer classes should be offered to high-level math students

Examples of policy propositions appropriate for secondary students would be:

1. Students should have a voice in hiring and firing of teachers
2. High school students should be allowed to eat lunch off campus
3. Physical education should be an elective course

Note: To be propositions of policy, these topics must indicate a change from the status quo and contain the word "should."

The two opposing sides in a debate are designated as the *affirmative* and the *negative*. The affirmative supports the proposition of policy. It agrees with the resolution about "what should be." The negative opposes the proposition of policy. It disagrees with the resolution. Each debater tries to present the best arguments and support for his or her assigned position regardless of personal beliefs on the issue. Each of the opposing sides attempts to persuade the observers to accept its point of view on the issue. The debaters accomplish this by presenting the best possible case for their own position and by pointing out flaws or deficiencies in the opposing side's position.

Each of the teams, affirmative and negative, will use the debate to present its views with supporting evidence and to attack the views and supporting evidence of the opposing side. The team members' views in the debate should be consistent with the overall position of their side, although each person will have special responsibilities. The responsibilities of the team members are as follows:

First Affirmative	• introduces topic
	• outlines what the team will attempt to prove
	• attempts to show a need for change
First Negative	• attempts to show that the present system is adequate and effective
Second Affirmative	• presents a plan
	• attempts to show that the plan is practical
	• attempts to show the plan is desirable
Second Negative	• attempts to show that the plan is not practical
	• attempts to show that the plan is not desirable

The role of the affirmative.   In essence the affirmative is saying "yes" to the proposition. The affirmative advocates a change from the status quo and recommends a policy to be adopted. The *first* responsibility of the affirmative is to clarify the meaning of the proposition. This is accomplished by *defining any ambiguous terms.* There is no need to define terms that are clearly understood, but words should be defined if there is any doubt about the meaning. For example, in the proposition "The United States should have a balanced budget," there is no need to define the term "United States" because its meaning is clear. The term "balanced budget" is an appropriate term for definition because we are not sure what that phrase means. The affirmative may define terms in several ways, including definition by authority, example, explanation, etymlogy, negation, or some combination of these.

The next responsibility of the affirmative is to present a *prima facie case* for their position. Because the affirmative recommends a change in the status quo, the affirmative has a special burden of proof. This means that the affirmative must present ample evidence in the first speech that on the face of it (on first appearance), the status quo is shown as undesirable, and the need for a change is established. If the affirmative does not present a prima facie case, the debate should stop there, for the negative has already won the debate without saying a word.

In presenting their prima facie case, the affirmative needs to isolate important issues, formulate these into contentions, and then substantiate these contentions with evidence and logic. An issue in debate is any main question of fact or theory which will help determine the final decision. These issues are essential to the proposition, which stands or falls according to how these issues are decided. An issue is not merely a question over which there is disagreement; only those questions which are crucial to the resolution are issues.

The stock (standard) issues in a debate involving a proposition of policy are as follows: (1) *Need* — is there a need for change? (2) *Solvency* — is the affirmative method of change (the plan) workable? Will it solve the need? (3) *Advantages* — if the plan goes into effect will it result in more benefits (advantages) than detriments (disadvantages)? All these issues need to be presented by the affirmative to complete their prima facie case. If there is no need to change, a need to change but no method to solve the need, or if there is a need and a method to solve the need but it would result in greater disadvantages than advantages, there is no need to debate the proposition. The affirmative wants to present a case which *shows a need* and a *workable method for solving the need* that results in a *better system* than the status quo.

The formulation of these issues into contentions is the next step. A contention is a general statement supporting or attacking a proposition. For example, in the resolution "The United States should have a balanced budget," a contention in support of the proposition might be that such a policy is desirable because it would decrease inflation. The affirmative could structure a prima facie case on this resolution with the following contentions: Contention 1 — Deficit spending causes inflation *(need)*; Contention 2 — A balanced budget would slow inflation and strengthen the dollar *(solvency)*; Contention 3 — A balanced budget would help the economy and increase government efficiency with money *(advantages)*. The student would support this general statement with evidence and logic to back it up — for example, with evidence showing how the national debt, brought about by deficit spending, has led (statistically) and will lead (in terms of probability) to inflation. The debater would also want to show why decreasing inflation is a desirable goal (because it helps people on fixed incomes, because it increases buying power, etc.). The negative will formulate contentions opposing the proposition. Using the same resolution, the negative might contend that balanced budgets would decrease money available for social programs and thus hurt the poor. They would likewise support this contention with specific evidence.

After an affirmative team has shown with their general contentions and supporting evidence that there is a *need* for change from the status quo, they must introduce a specific proposal to solve the need. The plan need not be very detailed, but the affirmative must show that their plan is *workable* and *advantageous*. In some topics, "need" becomes the key issue. In the example we have been dealing with, that of a balanced budget, the issue of whether we need a balanced budget would be the main issue, since once given the need, the plan is quite easy to formulate. In other topics the main issue becomes the workability rather than the desirability of the plan. For example, with a topic which proposes the adoption of some international organization to control weapons and ensure peace, it is not difficult to show the desirability of the plan. The challenge is to devise a plan that is workable.

It is important for both sides in the debate to examine the spin-off effects of the plan. Those secondary effects which are benefits of the plan will be presented by the affirmative as advantages. Those secondary effects which are detrimental will be presented by the negative as disadvantages.

Thus, the duties of the affirmative (in the constructive speeches) are (1) to define the proposition, (2) to show that the status quo is undesirable and justify a change from the present system (need), (3) show that the proposed plan is workable (solvency) and (4) that the proposed plan has advantages over the present system (desirability).

The role of the negative. The negative team opposes the proposition on the basis that the present system is adequate and effective. They are essentially saying "no" to the debate resolution. Their stance is that there is no need to adopt the affirmative proposal. The negative defends the present system (the status quo), refutes the affirmative need, and attacks the plan proposed as being unworkable and/or undesirable.

The negative strategy is one of *direct refutation*—direct denial of the affirmative case. This refutation takes the form of (1) attacking the affirmative presentation and (2) presenting counterargumentation.

In refuting the affirmative case, the negative attempts to bring out flaws in affirmative evidence and logic, showing that the evidence is inadequate or the reasoning defective. Evidence can be examined for flaws regarding date, qualifications, bias, consistency, and accuracy. If the affirmative uses a study on inflation to support a contention, for example, we would want to know if the study was conducted recently. If the study was completed in the 1920s, it may no longer be applicable. An author who makes a statement on an issue may have a different opinion many years later. In both these cases the evidence may be flawed because it is *outdated*.

If the affirmative uses a quotation from an expert or an authority as evidence, the negative may question whether the individual is qualified to speak on that subject. A physicist may be an excellent scientist, but this will not make the physicist qualified to speak on international relations. Similarly, a famous movie star should not be used as an authority in the area of economics. Many of the articles in popular magazines and newspapers are written by staff reporters who have no special expertise in the area. Thus, it is important to examine the *qualifications* of the alleged authority.

The negative will also want to determine if the authority is biased or prejudiced. Heads of major corporations may be well qualified to speak on business subjects, but a statement from them that antitrust laws are too strict and should be relaxed is flawed evidence because of their obvious bias.

The negative should examine the *consistency* of the evidence. The evidence may be equivocal. For example, a statement that an author *thinks* there is a *chance* that inflation *may* rise a *little* is not as strong or reliable as a statement that ten years of research have statistically shown that inflation will rise at five percent per year. It is important to determine the strength and nature of the opinion. Other evidence may not refer directly to the authority. Statements such as "It is known that Mr. X believes" or "From Mr. X's book one may conclude that his beliefs are'' do not represent the actual views of the authority. The debater may be imposing his or her own views upon the authority.

Finally, the negative should consider the *accuracy* of the evidence, particularly when statistics or studies are used. If the affirmative employs statistics to support an argument, the negative will want to ask whether the statistics were gathered scientifically and whether they are complete. For example, if the affirmative claims that ninety percent of renters favor rent control, a figure based on the affirmative side having asked ten of their friends and finding that nine agreed, the negative can easily attack this evidence on the grounds that it was not gathered scientifically.

No evidence is perfect. It is virtually impossible to find current, unbiased, consistent, and accurate information by well-qualified sources. This is merely a goal or ideal for both teams and a guide for comparing evidence. In choosing the evidence to support one's position, one will want to choose the most current, most qualified, least biased, most consistent, and most accurate information one can find. One also will be able to employ these evidence standards to compare evidence during the debate. If the affirmative presents a study on inflation, the negative now has a means to argue that their study on inflation is superior because it is more current, from a less biased source, more statistically sound, etc.

The affirmative has an opportunity to define the topic. If they do not do so, or if they define the proposition in an unreasonable way, the negative may offer their own definitions. For example, if the topic refers to the United States and the affirmative defines this as the United States of Brazil, the negative has legitimate grounds to object that this is an unreasonable interpretation of the term, and that it actually means the United States of America.

Having discussed direct refutation, we will now present counterargumentation related to classroom debate. The negative may deny the *need* isolated by the affirmative. The negative attempts to defend the status quo and show that the present system is adequate or desirable. In other words, the negative shows that there is no need to change from the present system because the status quo is sufficient. The negative can accomplish this by showing that the advantages of the present system outweigh the alleged disadvantages, that the affirmative attack on the status quo is not true or valid, or that the present system (even given its disadvantages) is still superior to that of the affirmative proposal.

In addition to attacking the affirmative need area, the negative may attack the *workability* of the affirmative plan. This can be accomplished by showing that the assets are insufficient, that compliance will not take place, or that the anticipated results will not occur. If the proposed plan is very expensive, it may not have adequate resources to work. If the plan is very unpopular or if there are loopholes, there may be only limited compliance with the plan. Prohibition is a good example of noncompliance. The Prohibition laws did not work effectively to decrease drinking because the compliance level was so low. The negative may also question whether the results projected by the affirmative will actually occur. The affirmative may have exaggerated the results or been overly optimistic about the effects of their plan. Perhaps there are important differences between past examples that will keep the affirmative plan from accomplishing its goals. These are strategies the negative can employ to deny the affirmative advantages.

Finally, the negative may defend the status quo by showing that the affirmative plan, even if it solved the alleged "evils" of the present system, would result in even more "evils" (disadvantages) than those in the status quo.

In sum, by attacking affirmative evidence and logic and by presenting counterarguments, the negative attempts to refute the affirmative case and defend the status quo.

Rebuttal speeches. Each team has two constructive speeches in which to initiate argumentation. After the constructive speeches, each team has two additional speeches designated as the rebuttals. In the rebuttals, the debaters cannot introduce any new contentions, but they can strengthen those already introduced. These rebuttals serve a somewhat different function from the constructive speeches. As with constructive speeches, the debaters will try to rebuild their case and refute the argument of the opposition. In addition, the rebuttal speakers will want to focus the debate on a *few critical issues* and lastly to summarize the overall position of the team.

The following is an outline of the steps just described, reflecting the time allotments and specific responsibilities for the debate team members.

The Two-on-Two Debate Format

The First Affirmative Constructive Speech (7 minutes)
   Addresses the people present and introduces topic
   Defines the terms
   Gives a one- or two-sentence history of the question
   Briefly states what the affirmative intends to prove
   Clearly states each contention
   Adequately supports each contention by example, statistics, authority, analogy, etc.
   Summarizes the affirmative's contentions at the conclusion of the talk

The First Negative Constructive Speech (7 minutes)
   Addresses the people present
   Accepts or redefines the definition of terms given by the first affirmative speaker
   Refutes the major issues raised by the affirmative
   Clearly states each negative contention
   Adequately supports each contention by example, statistics, authority, analogy, etc.

Summarizes the negative's position at the conclusion of the talk

The Second Affirmative Constructive Speech (7 minutes)
Addresses the people present
Restates and resubstantiates the contentions presented by the debater's partner
Answers the negative attack
Clearly states and explains the affirmative plan
Supports the desirability and feasibility of the plan with example, statistics, authority, analogy, etc.
Summarizes the affirmative's case at the conclusion of the talk

The Second Negative Constructive Speech (7 minutes)
Addresses the people present
Restates and resubstantiates contentions presented by the debater's partner
Answers the affirmative attack
Attacks the affirmative plan with example, statistics, authority, analogy, etc.
Summarizes the negative's case at the conclusion of the talk

The First Negative Rebuttal (3 minutes)
States each affirmative contention being refuted
Disproves each affirmative contention with logic and evidence
Balances time between refutation and summary

The First Affirmative Rebuttal (3 minutes)
States each negative contention being refuted
Disproves each negative contention with logic and evidence
Balances time between refutation and summary

The Second Negative Rebuttal (3 minutes)
States the affirmative contention being refuted
Disproves the affirmative's contentions by example, statistics, authority, analogy, etc.
Summarizes the negative's case by demonstrating there is no need to change the status quo
Summarizes the negative's case by showing the affirmative plan will not meet its alleged need
Summarizes the negative's case by showing the affirmative's plan is a poorer alternative than the status quo

The Second Affirmative Rebuttal (3 minutes)
States the negative's contention being refuted
Disproves the negative's contention by example, statistics, authority, analogy, etc.
Summarizes the affirmative's case by demonstrating there is a need for a change
Summarizes the affirmative's case by showing the plan meets this need
Summarizes the affirmative's case by showing that the affirmative's plan is a better alternative than the status quo

Figure 7–1. CHECKLIST FOR IMPLEMENTING ADVOCACY LEARNING

Have you:

_____ 1. Selected a topic (or topics) for a classroom debate reflecting the personal, social, and/or academic needs and interests of your students?

_____ 2. Determined that the topic(s) are appropriate for the grade level of your students?

_____ 3. Set up the debate teams, consisting of two affirmative speakers and two negative speakers per team?

_____ 4. Explained the functions of the teams to the entire class?

_____ 5. Provided guidance to the debaters as they prepared their cases?

_____ 6. Provided roles for the audience members who will listen to the debate?

_____ 7. Held a discussion/debriefing session with the entire class after the debate?

_____ 8. Elicited student feedback regarding the success or lack of success of the debate?

_____ 9. Determined the outcome of the debate, if applicable, in terms of the academic growth of the students?

_____ 10. Evaluated the overall strengths and weaknesses of the debate using teacher comments and notes taken during the debate?

Although the debate format may at first seem more suitable for secondary students, the authors have worked with elementary students using this instructional strategy with great success. One debate, conducted by sixth-graders, focused on an issue of particular concern to the students: establishing an after-school soccer team for girls only. The interest developed when the existing sports program did not satisfy the needs of all participants; because there were four girls and twelve boys on the original team, the girls believed they did not get adequate playing time. A debate was proposed as a way of clarifying the issues and as a means for deciding what ought to be done.

The teams prepared their debates, establishing contentions supporting their views. The affirmative team focused the need for change from the current situation and proposed a plan. The negative prepared a case for maintaining the status quo and sought to find weaknesses in the affirmative plan.

The members of the class who did not actually participate in presenting the debate had specific functions to perform during the debate; they took notes on the debate and critiqued the speeches using assessment forms. Upon completion of the debate, a vote was taken by the whole class to determine the resolution of the issue.

Thus, the students developed many valuable skills, including skills in written and oral communication, listening, analyzing, and critical thinking, while they explored a topic of personal and social significance to the group.

Figure 7–1 is a checklist to aid teachers in implementing advocacy training.

CHAPTER SUMMARY

In this chapter, we have provided an introduction to the instructional strategy of advocacy learning along with the steps necessary for implementation in the classroom. The range of possible debate topics is as broad as the interests and areas of concern represented at the elementary and secondary levels. This student-centered instructional approach yields many positive results as students gain experience and confidence in the art of argumentation.

CHAPTER EIGHT

TECHNOLOGY IN THE CLASSROOM

The preceding chapters have presented a range of curricular decisions and instructional strategies which represent a broad-based repertoire for the classroom teacher. Turning now to technology, we are presented with an external force which does not allow much flexibility in content but certainly falls into the realm of teacher-based decision making. In this light, technology is not an intrusive force which competes with the teacher but rather represents another forum through which to reach students and meet their needs.

TECHNOLOGICAL RESOURCES

We will be referring to the following types of technology in this discussion: audiovisual media (film, filmstrips, television, and videocassettes) and computers. Although other forms of technology may be used in the classroom, these are the forms which seem to be the most pervasive and offer the widest range of instructional support. These types of technology will be presented in terms of their impact on instructional decision making:

1. *Audiovisual media*—application to learning principles; instructional uses
2. *Computers*—classroom uses; types of software; guidelines for software selection

Film, filmstrips, television, and videocassette recorders are considered to be *noninteractive* media because the viewer cannot alter the presentation. It

is the same over time, the only variations coming from the quality of the production, that is, sound quality and picture clarity. These media are employed
most effectively in the classroom where they are selected to support a specific
instructional objective; this may be a cognitive or affective objective. They
may be used as a part of a one-time lesson or used as a series throughout a
designed unit. There are a myriad of educational audiovisual resources
available to teachers; depending on budgetary constraints, district resources,
and the instructional needs of students, such resources can successfully serve
to augment certain instructional sequences.

RATIONALE FOR CLASSROOM USE

One way to view the pedagogical rationale for using these media in the
classroom is to apply their use to basic learning principles (discussed in detail
in Chapter 2). Films, filmstrips, television, and videocassette recorders may
lend support to several important learning principles through providing these
conditions: (1) To introduce an instructional sequence, they can establish an
anticipatory set for learning; (2) they incorporate left- and right- brain learning by presenting information through auditory and visual means; (3) they
can increase the motivation levels of students because they provide diversity
in the instructional sequence; with films and videos, especially, the medium
itself may be a motivating factor; and (4) they can provide an effective means
of viewing previously presented material, thus giving students appropriate
practice with concepts.

In addition to incorporating key learning principles into the educational
setting, audiovisual media have a variety of uses in the classroom. They may
be used to introduce a particular unit and establish a particular mood and
mind set for the topic(s) to be covered. For example: In a history class about
to cover the Great Depression, the film *The Grapes of Wrath* might be shown
to introduce the unit; the film would provide potentially long-lasting visual
images, generate questions, and create the tone for subsequent study. They
also may be used to conclude a particular unit and provide a sense of closure
of topics presented. For example: A videocassette of *The Scarlet Letter* may be
shown to an English class at the conclusion of the American literature unit.

Audiovisual media may be used effectively to reinforce key concepts and
ideas during a unit and to strengthen students' understanding of material
which has been presented orally or in a text. For example: A television
documentary on drug abuse may be shown in a health class to reinforce key
concepts being covered. Additionally, it may be used to promote discussion
on a topic being studied in class. For example: In a fifth-grade class, students
studying endangered species may view a filmstrip on two endangered
creatures and then discuss their reactions.

Such media may provide opportunities to further affective objectives in
the instructional sequence. For example: In an English class, students study-

ing the poetry of Robert Frost may watch a film which combines readings of his poems and visual imagery to accompany them. Students increase their awareness and appreciation of the art of poetry through such viewing. And lastly, these media may be used to increase creativity in the classroom. For example: Students may view a videocassette dealing with outer space and be asked to write an original science fiction short story based on their visual impressions and reactions.

Although the preceding list is not exhaustive, it reflects the range of ways that audiovisual resources may be used to strengthen the instructional sequence. It is essential to preview any piece before classroom use to ensure that it is appropriate for the age and the social and intellectual levels of one's students. In addition, it is important to formulate broad-based goals and specific objectives for any piece to ensure its sound incorporation into the students' educational experience.

We advocate the use of audiovisual review teams to preview the resources; such teams usually consist of teachers and students. Summaries of the works are made and kept cataloged, usually in the school library. If particular television documentaries are especially appropriate and well done, video libraries can be established at the school or district level; copyright laws must be noted and adhered to. Local libraries generally have catalogs of films and often other audiovisual resources; this can be a helpful resource for teachers.

In sum, audiovisual resources, when used effectively and selectively, can serve to increase students' willingness to learn, improve their attitude toward targeted content, and strengthen the processing and retention of key concepts being studied.

COMPUTERS IN THE CLASSROOM

In contrast to audiovisual media, computers are an *interactive* medium, whereby the student has the opportunity to interact with and somehow affect or alter the presented sequence. It has in common with audiovisual resources the ability to increase student motivation and to present information and ideas through visual and auditory stimuli. In addition, computers provide students with a kinesthetic experience through the use of the computer keyboard.

There are three primary uses of computers in the classroom: (1) to teach students to become computer literate, (2) to teach the fundamentals of computer programming and problem-solving, and (3) to serve as an instructional aid.

Because of their extensive use in businesses, schools, and homes, computers are fast becoming a major technological presence in society. Many contend that computer literacy constitutes an important educational goal and should be incorporated into the standard curriculum at the elementary and secondary levels. There are several different approaches which may be taken to introduce students to the world of computers. Some examples are: (1) computer labs may be established, students visiting the lab on a rotating basis, according to a fixed schedule; (2) each classroom may have a certain number of computers, and students may rotate through a learning center on its use, or the computers may be used on an as-needed basis; (3) specific academic departments may house the majority of the school's computers (i.e., English and Math), and students receive basic computer instruction applied to the designated academic subject. Depending upon the financial resources of the district and the commitment to foster computer literacy, the resultant educational programs may take a variety of forms in implementation.

Teaching the fundamentals of computer programming and problem solving is an extension of computer literacy. It involves teaching students computer languages and applying them in some cases to subject matter. For example, students may acquire computer languages such as Basic or LOGO to learn mathematical content. At this stage of computer instruction, student-generated theories and problems may be fed into the computer for feedback. Many believe that this process strengthens critical thinking skills, logic, and problem solving.

A third major way for computers to be used in the classroom is as an instructional aid, commonly called Computer Aided Instruction (CAI). Such instruction is considered to be a supplement to the on-going classroom instruction; it offers another vehicle by which students may acquire information and skills and receive direct assistance.

CAI programs are available and can be developed for most curriculum areas. A representative, although not nearly exhaustive, list of CAI curricular applications follows:

1. reading comprehension
2. vocabulary development
3. punctuation
4. paragraph writing
5. arithmetic operations
6. monetary concepts
7. map reading
8. reference skills
9. historical data
10. graphics

The versatility and classroom usefulness of such programs are readily apparent. The key is to select and implement such programs wisely, within a well-planned instructional framework.

There are four basic types of CAI software which are currently available: (1) drill-and-practice, (2) tutorials, (3) simulations, and (4) computer-managed instruction. *Drill-and-practice* is the type which is used most extensively in the classroom. Typically, these programs display problems, and the student responds by selecting among provided responses. The computer indicates if a correct or incorrect response has been given. In such programs, the instructional intent is to provide the student with appropriate practice within a specific content area and provide quick and accurate knowledge of results. Drill-and-practice programs must be matched with the students' ability levels and instructional needs. The appropriate level of difficulty is required for the practice exercises to be worthwhile. Also, a program should provide good visual reinforcement to enliven the sequence; auditory reinforcement also helps to maintain interest and sustain attention over time. Incorrect responses, when selected by students, should lead to some sort of appropriate help sequence for the learner.

In contrast with drill-and-practice programs, which strengthen skills and review previously encountered concepts, *tutorial* programs introduce new content to students and may provide drill-and-practice sequences as followup. Generally, such programs provide a pretest and posttest related to the presented content. They are usually used for enrichment in the classroom; also, they may present content which the student has missed because of absence. Additionally, some tutorials are used as a review of presented material to check for understanding and increase retention of concepts.

Simulations constitute another type of computer software. Typically, real-life situations are presented to the student, outlining a set of corresponding conditions. Students then make decisions and determine the consequences for these decisions. Examples of formats for simulations are: (1) political issues, for example, nuclear power, (2) pioneer life, and (3) family dilemmas. For experience-based instruction in the classroom, such simulation sequences offer a close facsimile to real-life decision-making situations.

Computer-managed instruction refers to computer software which keeps track of student progress within a designated instructional sequence. It provides cross-referencing with other programs when more extensive practice or assistance is needed . These programs measure students' skills, record scores, and correlate data with those of other students.

GUIDELINES FOR COMPUTER SOFTWARE SELECTION

The following guidelines are provided for a more in-depth look at criteria for software selection:

1. Determine the specific instructional needs of the students who will be using the software. Careful planning should take place to decide who will use the software and under what instructional conditions. Because of budgeting factors, the program with the greatest applicability to those in greatest need should be sought.

2. It is more effective, although initially very time consuming, to have a review team run the program prior to purchase. Both teachers and students

should participate in such reviews. District curriculum specialists, if available, may be able to provide assistance in this process. Evaluation forms should be devised for this review and applied to it.

3. The quality of the program needs to be considered. The visuals should be appropriate and engaging. The printed message should be clear and readable.

4. The material should be highly interactive, allowing the student to be actively involved in the instructional sequence.

5. Consider teacher time that the program requires. If lengthy introductions and explanations and considerable teacher assistance are called for, the program may not be able to be used often or efficiently.

The following "Software Program Evaluation Form" translates these five criteria into a software evaluation format. The completed form provides a sample of the evaluation applied to a computer software program.

SOFTWARE PROGRAM EVALUATION

Program Name: _____

Subject Area: _____ Grade Level: _____

1. INSTRUCTIONAL OBJECTIVES OF PROGRAM

    _____
    _____
    _____
    _____
    _____
    _____

   INSTRUCTIONAL NEEDS OF STUDENTS ADDRESSED BY PROGRAM

    _____
    _____
    _____
    _____
    _____
    _____

   CONDITIONS FOR USE

    _____
    _____
    _____
    _____
    _____
    _____

2. TO EVALUATE THIS PROGRAM, A TEAM COULD:

    _____
    _____
    _____
    _____

_____

_____

3. QUALITY OF THE PROGRAM

_____

_____

_____

_____

_____

_____

4. INTERACTIVE QUALITY OF PROGRAM

_____

_____

_____

_____

_____

_____

5. TEACHER TIME AND ASSISTANCE REQUIRED

_____

_____

_____

_____

_____

_____

6. OTHER COMMENTS

_____

_____

_____

_____

_____

SOFTWARE PROGRAM EVALUATION

Program Name: Story Machine, Spinnaker, 1982

Subject Area: Elementary English   Grade Level: K–4

1. INSTRUCTIONAL OBJECTIVES OF PROGRAM

   STATED: Develop story-writing ability. Increase vocabulary development. Increase sight vocabulary. Increase grammar awareness. Improve attitude toward writing. Increase keyboard familiarity.
   REVIEWER-DETERMINED OBJECTIVES: Increase motivation to write.
   Increase simple spelling ability. Reinforce basic grammatical structures.

   INSTRUCTIONAL NEEDS OF STUDENTS ADDRESSED BY PROGRAM

   Would assist resistant writers in creating simple sentences and building
   simple stories. Students with short attention spans may be motivated by
   accompanying visuals which act out the simple sentences. Students with
   low frustration level may not do well with the program because adequate help sequences are not provided. Students need to have basic
   understanding of grammatical structure in order to follow instructions.

   CONDITIONS FOR USE

   Because program limitations are fairly extensive, students would need
   training in how to use the program. Individuals, as opposed to groups,
   would use the program. Booklet to accompany the disk is necessary to
   complete the program. Time on the program would range from 10 to 30
   minutes. Prior instruction is needed to cover grammatical concepts,
   especially parts of speech.

2. TO EVALUATE THIS PROGRAM, A TEAM COULD:

   Run the program and make mistakes to see the approach to correcting
   mistakes. Program offers a sound or no-sound option and a white- or
   black-screen option; team should try both. Student reviewers should try
   the program independently and with teacher assistance to determine

necessary level of assistance. Team should look at the program holistically to determine if the program indeed enhances story-writing ability. May have other actual benefits.

3. QUALITY OF THE PROGRAM

The text is readable and generally well spaced on the screen; half is the text which is being written and half is the visual component. The student assistance is good and appropriately placed. The visuals are clear and relate well to the text.

4. INTERACTIVE QUALITY OF PROGRAM

The program calls for a fairly high level of interaction but is limiting in terms of potential input. Only a relatively small number of words can be used to create sentences. The help sequences seem somewhat limited. Several grammatical restrictions are placed on sentence formation which may hinder certain story-writing skills.

5. TEACHER TIME AND ASSISTANCE REQUIRED

Considering the designated age group, substantial teacher involvement would be required, especially for 5- to 7-year-olds. There are several limitations which would need to be explained. Because of the help sequences, the teacher might be summoned frequently during the sequence.

6. OTHER COMMENTS

If a key instructional objective in the given classroom is story writing, it is this reviewer's opinion that this program would not meet the needs of most students related to the objectives. However, if students need practice in forming simple sentences, the program could be useful on a limited basis.

CHAPTER SUMMARY

In this chapter we have discussed the potential benefits of incorporating audiovisual media and computers into curricular planning. We outlined how learning principles are promoted through the use of audiovisual resources and provided examples which reveal the versatility of such resources. It was recommended that teachers form teams to investigate and preview available audiovisual media; such effort seems well worthwhile in light of the perceived benefits to students. The important new frontier of computer literacy was highlighted, and an overview of types of computer software was provided. We discussed how to select and evaluate available software programs and offered specific guidelines to aid in this process. Technology in the classroom broadens the range of formats for presenting content to students and comprises an important area of instructional design.

CHAPTER NINE

ASSESSING TEACHING PROFICIENCY: PLANNING AND EXECUTION

Teaching involves both careful planning and effective execution. In most of the preceding chapters, we have looked at the strategic act of teacher planning. However, an evaluator of teachers must attend not only to planning but to the execution of the teacher's written plans as well. In some cases a written plan may fall down upon execution; conversely, a lesson may become strengthened once it is executed.

This chapter makes concrete the underlying principles presented in the preceding chapters. Provided first are assessment instruments for the planning and execution of instruction. Next are sample elementary and secondary lesson plans and unit plans which were completed by students who were instructed in the approaches used in this book. These plans may be viewed as representative lesson and unit plans which would be appropriate at such a level of competence. The lessons and units are generally exemplary and incorporate the essential elements of sound instructional planning.

Because of the importance of assessment, typically done either by the teacher or an external evaluator, we have included the actual written feedback given to the students on their written plans. The questions used on the assessment instruments highlight those areas considered to be most crucial to instructional success.

As discussed in preceding chapters, written plans are an essential part of the instructional process. Lessons are presented daily and need to include the intended objectives, the relevant learning principles, and the means by which relative success will be gauged. Units are designed for longer time sequences and need to include the entire scope and sequence of the unit content. The careful initial planning required of both lessons and units is generally correlated to the successful implementation of the written plan.

Specifically, the assessment instruments which follow address (1) the strategic planning of lesson plans and teaching units, and (2) the quality of communication in an instructional sequence. An instructional sequence may be assessed through the use of either of these instruments or a combination of them, depending upon the evaluator's purpose for assessing the quality of instruction in a given classroom.

ASSESSING THE STRATEGIC PLANNING OF THE LESSON PLAN

Lesson Topic: _____ Grade Level: _____

1. INSTRUCTIONAL OBJECTIVES

a. Are the objectives stated operationally and in precise and measurable terms?
Yes _____ No _____

b. Are the objectives developmentally well chosen? Yes _____ No _____

Comments: _____

_____

_____

2. MATERIALS

a. Are the instructional materials appropriate for meeting the objectives?
Yes _____ No _____

b. Are the instructional materials adequate to provide accommodation to different learning styles? Yes _____ No _____

Comments: _____

_____

_____

3. MOTIVATION

a. Are the motivational techniques incorporated into the lesson adequate for generating an interest in the lesson? Yes _____ No _____

b. Are the motivational techniques incorporated into the lesson adequate in terms of maintaining and sustaining an interest in the lesson?
Yes _____ No _____

Comments: _____

_____

_____

4. PROCEDURE

a. Are the teacher and learner roles/activities during the lesson clearly outlined and explained? Yes _____ No _____

b. Are the activities in the instructional sequence congruent with the lesson's objectives? Yes _____ No _____

c. Is the lesson plan logically sequenced? Yes _____ No _____

d. Do the activities in the lesson provide for individual differences in learning?
Yes _____   No _____

e. Do the activities in the lesson represent clear examples of the effective use of learning principles?   Yes _____   No _____

Comments: _____

_____

_____

5. TIME ESTIMATES

a. Are the time estimates in the lesson appropriately paced?
Yes _____   No _____

b. Are the time estimates in the lesson realistic?   Yes _____   No _____

Comments: _____

_____

_____

6. EVALUATION

a. Is the evaluation of the lesson appropriate in terms of assessment of completed objectives?   Yes _____   No _____

b. Is the evaluation of the lesson appropriate in terms of assessment of the overall success of the lesson design?   Yes _____   No _____

Comments: _____

_____

_____

7. INDEPENDENT WORK AND FOLLOW-UP

a. If independent work is assigned, does such work provide appropriate practice to reinforce the stated objectives?
Yes _____   No _____   Not applicable _____

b. If follow-up assignments are included, do they enhance the stated goals of the lesson plan?   Yes _____   No _____   Not applicable _____

Comments: _____

_____

_____

_____

ASSESSING THE STRATEGIC PLANNING OF THE TEACHING UNIT

Lesson Topic: _____ Grade Level: _____

1. BACKGROUND INFORMATION
   a. Is the background information provided adequate for conveying the underlying philosophy of the unit? Yes _____   No _____
   b. Does the background information provide a concise profile of the learners?
      Yes _____   No _____

Comments: _____

_____

_____

_____

2. UNIT DESCRIPTION
   a. Does the unit description offer a clear explanation of the rationale for implementing the unit? Yes _____   No _____
   b. Are the goals and objectives of the unit:
      • Clearly stated? Yes _____   No _____
      • Comprehensive enough to support the planned scope of the unit?
        Yes _____   No _____

Comments: _____

_____

_____

_____

3. INSTRUCTIONAL PLAN
   a. Task Analysis. Is the task analysis complete in terms of providing:
      • A clear and sound assessment of entry-level behavior?
        Yes _____   No _____
      • Appropriate and comprehensive intermediate steps?
        Yes _____   No _____
      • A complete set of target behaviors which match the instructional objectives? Yes _____   No _____
   b. Activities. Are the scheduled activities:
      • Sufficiently comprehensive to achieve the planned objectives?
        Yes _____   No _____

- Presented in a logical sequence so as to maximize the achievement of the objective? Yes _____ No _____
- Clearly stated with sufficient amplification to provide a clear instructional picture of their intent? Yes _____ No _____

c. Sample Daily Lesson Plans. Does the sample daily lesson plan:

- Model a sound and comprehensive lesson plan? Yes _____ No _____
- Lead to the mastery of the stated objectives? Yes _____ No _____

Comments: _____

_____

_____

_____

4. RESOURCES AND INSTRUCTIONAL MATERIALS

Are the resources and instructional materials used in the unit:

- Comprehensive enough to support the unit? Yes _____ No _____
- Oriented toward a variety of learning styles? Yes _____ No _____

Comments: _____

_____

_____

_____

5. EVALUATION PROCEDURES

a. Preassessment. Is the preassessment planned for the unit:

- Appropriate for the learners? Yes _____ No _____
- Adequate for the planned objectives? Yes _____ No _____

b. Formative Evaluation. Are the criterion checks adequate to ensure on-going successful mastery of the unit objectives? Yes _____ No _____

c. Unit Evaluation. Does the unit evaluation:

- Include all target instructional objectives? Yes _____ No _____
- Provide for adequate teacher and student input?
  Yes _____ No _____

Comments: _____

_____

_____

ASSESSING THE QUALITY OF COMMUNICATION IN THE INSTRUCTIONAL SEQUENCE

1 = needs a great deal of work
2 = needs some work
3 = competent
4 = excels

1. Ethos of Sender (Poise, Security)

   1   2   3   4

Comments: _____

_____

_____

2. Ethos of Sender (Psychological Dominance)

   1   2   3   4

Comments: _____

_____

_____

3. Delivery: Voice

   1   2   3   4

Comments: _____

_____

_____

4. Delivery: Mannerisms

   1   2   3   4

Comments: _____

_____

_____

5. Digressions (Comfortable/Uncomfortable)

    1   2   3   4

Comments: _____

_____

_____

6. Clarity of Message (Explaining Content and Giving Directions)

    1   2   3   4

Comments: _____

_____

_____

7. Use of Concrete Examples

    1   2   3   4

Comments: _____

_____

_____

8. Effective Use of Repetition

    1   2   3   4

Comments: _____

_____

_____

9. Effective Use of Summarization (Formative/Summative)

    1   2   3   4

Comments: _____

_____

_____

ELEMENTARY LESSON PLAN

Lesson Topic: ___Writing a News Lead_____

Unit Topic: ___The Newspaper_____ Grade Level:___6_____

1. INSTRUCTIONAL OBJECTIVE
   The learner will write an effective news lead utilizing the five Ws and 1 H structure.

2. MATERIALS
   8½ x 11 papers labeled *Who, What, When, Where, Why,* and *How,* to be used to emphasize the usage of these question words in a news lead.

3. MOTIVATION
   Who can tell me what a line leader does? We call the first paragraph in a news story a news lead for the very same reason. A news lead leads us into the story just as a line leader leads us into the room. The lead helps us to know where we are going. It contains the most important information of the story all in one sentence! It should also capture your attention so you will want to read the rest of the story. Today we will learn about how to write a news lead [This lesson will actually take two days]. Here's an example: [uncover following paragraph written ahead on board]:

   "Room 13 eagerly learned how to write a news lead today in their classroom when their teacher told them it was an important concept to understand in their newspaper unit."

4. PROCEDURE
   Who would like to read this out loud? Joey . . . Everyone should be reading along with Joey because I will be asking some important questions after he is through. Five of my questions begin with W. If you answer correctly you will receive one of these cards [hand out as children respond].
   a. *Who* learned something? Underline answer in example.
   b. *What* did they learn?
   c. *When* did they learn?
   d. *Where* did they learn?
   e. *Why* did they learn?

   My last question does not begin with a W and it applies to a later example. Just remember the question *How?*

   Now, when I say a part of this lead, I'd like the person holding that W to come up to the front.
   a. Today
   b. Room 13, etc.

   Good! Let's say these five W's together . . . [say words in unison]. Remember, they are all words that begin with a question. Don't forget about poor old *How* [hold up]. We'll meet him later! A proper news lead should answer every question.

Here's another example [uncover]:

"On November 15, 1986, a boy from Carthay Center School ate seven hot fudge sundaes at the corner ice cream store in an effort to break the school record."

Mary—you were the *Who* last time. Please ask your question word to the class and then ask someone to answer it. If the student is correct, give him/her your card. The whole class should be thinking . . . [proceed through all cards].

Let's try one more [uncover]:

"The UCLA Bruins beat the USC Trojans 27 to 17 last Saturday at the Coliseum by scoring 21 points in the second half of the game."

When I say a part of the sentence, I would like you to raise one finger if it is a *Who* answer, two fingers if it is a *What* answer, etc.

[The cards will be up in front facing the students in numerical order. If most of the students can distinguish the answers, move on to independent work.]

5. TIME ESTIMATES

Motivation—5 minutes

Procedure—25 minutes for the first day. If a second day is necessary to ensure comprehension, 20 minutes should be allotted.

Independent Work—20 minutes.

6. EVALUATION

Was I clear and concise in the explanation of news leads? Did I give examples the students found interesting? Did the students seem motivated? Could they keep up with me and the concepts I was giving them? Did the students write leads that adhered to the structure I taught them?

7. INDEPENDENT WORK AND FOLLOW-UP

Hand out worksheet entitled "Follow the Lead!" (at end of lesson plan). Go over first example with the students and then walk around answering questions. Assign unfinished work for homework and add one more original lead to their assignment. Explain that we will review tomorrow (thus the two-day lesson) and that we will have more practice. Lower their level of concern! This might be a difficult concept.

Follow-up: Review concepts throughout the next week and a half. Use enrichment worksheets and incorporate upcoming unit topic of news stories.

FOLLOW THE LEAD!

Label the facts in numbers 1 and 2 below *Who, What, When, Where, Why,* and *How.* The problems may *not* contain an example of all six possible question words. After you have labeled them, write a news lead using the facts. Remember—be informative *and* exciting! For number 3, write your own set of facts and an original news lead using them.

1. a. He was invited by the school to discuss crime
   b. A policeman
   c. Yesterday
   d. In the auditorium
   e. To talk to sixth-graders

2. a. Last week
   b. Voted
   c. 100 sixth-graders
   d. In the cafeteria
   e. In order to support the candidates

3. Write your own news lead. Write down your facts first, label them, and then write your lead. This is your chance to *lead* your way to becoming a famous journalist. Good luck!

_____

_____

_____

_____

_____

_____

_____

_____

ASSESSING THE STRATEGIC PLANNING OF THE LESSON PLAN

Lesson Topic: ___Writing a News Lead___ Grade Level:___Sixth___

1. INSTRUCTIONAL OBJECTIVES

a. Are the objectives stated operationally and in precise and measurable terms?
Yes __X__ No _____

b. Are the objectives developmentally well chosen? Yes __X__ No _____

Comments: "Behavior" and "content" are clearly presented by the objective.

The "domain" or situation in which the knowledge is to apply is not given.

We suggest the following revision: "Given a set of facts related to a news

story, the learner will be able to write an effective news lead utilizing

the five Ws and 1 H structure."

2. MATERIALS

a. Are the instructional materials appropriate for meeting the objectives?
Yes __X__ No _____

b. Are the instructional materials adequate to provide accommodation to different learning styles? Yes __X__ No _____

Comments: Through the materials (cards labeled with the five Ws), both

visual and verbal strategies are utilized. Use of question cards allows dif-

ferent response modes (oral, raising fingers). Thus, different learning

styles are accommodated.

3. MOTIVATION

a. Are the motivational techniques incorporated into the lesson adequate in terms of generating an interest in the lesson? Yes __X__ No _____

b. Are the motivational techniques incorporated into the lesson adequate in terms of maintaining and sustaining an interest in the lesson?
Yes __X__ No _____

Comments: The use of the line leader analogy is quite clever. The use-

fulness of the material is made evident to the learners. The example leads

are relevant to the interests of sixth-graders and should maintain and

sustain interest in the lesson itself.

4. PROCEDURE
   a. Are the teacher and learner roles/activities during the lesson clearly outlined and explained?
      Yes __X__ No _____ (*See Comments)
   b. Are the activities in the instructional sequence congruent with the lesson's objectives? Yes __X__ No _____ (**See Comments)
   c. Is the lesson plan logically sequenced? Yes __X__ No _____
   d. Do the activities in the lesson provide for individual differences in learning?
      Yes __X__ No _____
   e. Do the activities in the lesson represent clear examples of the effective use of learning principles? Yes __X__ No _____

Comments: Learning principles—appropriate practice (with additions see **),
immediate feedback or knowledge of results, positive reinforcement, active
learning, moving from the known to the unknown, logical sequencing,
mnemonics (five Ws, 1 H), etc.—are well utilized. Overall, the lesson has been
thoughtfully planned.

    *Are questions 1 to 5 in Procedure section 4 supposed to be asked orally,
written on the blackboard, or written on the cards? Until reading section 5, I
thought only the five Ws were written on the cards. We are not clear on one
minor point.

    **All the activities given are prerequisites, but one major addition to the
instructional sequence needs to be made before total congruence is achieved.

    Your ultimate goal is for students to be able to write their own leads, but,
before assigning independent work, you never give students practice in writing original leads. This is easily remedied. Before moving on to independent
work, the teacher should give several sets of five facts (five Ws) to the class
and should have the class compose original leads based on these facts.

5. TIME ESTIMATES

a. Are the time estimates in the lesson appropriately paced?
Yes __X__ No _____

b. Are the time estimates in the lesson realistic? Yes __X__ No _____

Comments: If our addition to the instructional sequence (see preceding Comments section) is incorporated, procedure time may need to be expanded by 5 or 10 minutes. Frequent changes in terms of student response mode (oral, raising fingers) and in question form (asking for the corresponding fact or asking for the corresponding W) should also help hold students' attention throughout the 30-minute teacher-directed portion of the lesson.

6. EVALUATION:

a. Is the evaluation of the lesson appropriate in terms of assessment of completed objectives? Yes __X__ No _____

b. Is the evaluation of the lesson appropriate in terms of assessment of the overall success of the lesson design? Yes __X__ No _____

Comments: Perhaps section 6 ("Evaluation") should mention that the worksheet ("Follow the Lead") will be graded and returned with comments. This fact is mentioned in Independent work section VII but needs to be noted here as well.

7. INDEPENDENT WORK AND FOLLOW-UP:

a. If independent work is assigned, does such work provide appropriate practice to reinforce the stated objectives?
Yes __X__ No _____ Not applicable _____

b. If follow-up assignments are included, do they enhance the stated goals of the lesson plan? Yes __X__ No _____ Not applicable _____

Comments: Appropriate practice and spaced review are provided.

SECONDARY LESSON PLAN

Lesson Topic: __Negation: Review of Vocabulary__

Unit Topic: __Spanish I__   Grade Level: __High School__

1. INSTRUCTIONAL OBJECTIVE

The goal of the lesson is to present and practice the negation and review past vocabulary.

The objectice will be implied, but not directly stated to the students. The objective will be specified for them at the end of the lesson.

The learner will:

- respond to review questions using appropriate grammar and vocabulary
- hear the introduction to the negation as modeled by the teacher (Q/A)
- respond to a question using the negation (with prompting from the teacher, if needed)
- write selected sentences on the board and in notes
- read and correct these sentences
- extract/state the rule for the negation with the guidance of the teacher
- copy the rule for the formation of the negation from the board into additional notes.
- correctly answer questions using the negation; practice use of the negative
- interview another student, asking questions that will elicit a negative response
- write the interview on a sheet of paper and turn it in
- respond to various questions asked by the teacher using correct grammar and vocabulary in order to win a tic-tac-toe space
- look at posters and pictures

Homework: transform affirmative sentences into the negation; answer questions using the negation

2. MATERIALS

The students will write answers and sentences on the blackboard. *Objects* in the room, *pictures,* and *posters* will be used to initiate both affirmative and negative responses to specific questions.

3. MOTIVATION

Oral praise will be given: *bueno, perfecto, excelente.* Immediate knowledge of their performance will be given. Questions will be directed toward their interests, traits, and current events in a game format. The opportunity will be given to write their sentences on the board as a reward for the correct use of the negation. The teacher may also opt to initially stimulate interest in the topic by rhetorically asking the students, ''How would you tell me that you aren't Spanish?''

Slow learners: Extra time and more prompts will be provided for these students. The responses of the other students will provide them with models. They will have the reinforcement of mass practice/response. They will be asked easier questions. During the interview session, slower students will be paired with advanced students who can help them ask and answer questions.

Advanced learners: The teacher will ask them more "difficult" questions. They may be asked to correct others. They will be asked to indicate the rule.

4 . PROCEDURE

Anticipatory Set: "Buenos días!" Question-answer period reviewing past material covered.

Input Modalities: Oral, written, and visual. Discovery lesson. The teacher will present the concept in Spanish. The students will respond using the negative. The students will write on the board with the teacher's aid. They will read and correct these sentences and then deduce the rule.

Model: The teacher will orally demonstrate the concept and will write a sentence in the negation on the board if this is needed.

Checking/Evaluation: The teacher will check and evaluate comprehension during the presentation phase through question and answer, correcting mistakes, and using certain students as models (after they have demonstrated competency). The teacher may lengthen or shorten this period depending on student performance.

Guided-Practice: Done simultaneously with above. There will also be a period at the end of the lesson when the students will ask questions in pairs and correct themselves as the teacher circulates. It is also during this phase of the lesson that the teacher may evaluate how well the concept was learned and determine if any adjustments need to be made in the following plans or in the approaches used.

Activities: Review of exam and past concepts and vocabulary. Presentation of negative *orally* (question-answer) and *written* form (on board, in notes). *Games:* Interview between two students using the negative; a tic-tac-toe match game, with one side of the class competing against the other.

5. TIME ESTIMATES
Indicated on the script of the plan, next page.

6. EVALUATION
Did I vary the reinforcement? Was the pacing appropriate? When did the students seem most and/or least interested? Was there enough time for the students to benefit from the game? Did they feel lost? Should I have delayed the interview to the following day? Did the students act/look as though they were rushed or overloaded? Were any students upset when they were corrected by me or by other students? Were my transitions smooth?

7. INDEPENDENT WORK AND FOLLOW-UP
Homework exercises given. Correction of homework in class the following day. Review and practice of the negative during the following days.

SCRIPT TO ACCOMPANY LESSON

1. Buenos días, clase (2–5 minutes).

   ¿Cuál es la fecha de hoy?

   ¿Qué día es hoy?

   ¿Cuáles son los días de la semana?

   Cuenta de 1 a 20 (flash cards).

   Enseña una fotografía—¿cómo es X? ¿Es grande, pequeña, bonita, inteligente, etc.?

2. La Negación (20 minutes)

Teacher:	¿Qué es eso?
Student:	Un cuadro, un escritorio, un libro, un estudiante, una bolsa.
Teacher:	¿Dónde está X?
Teacher:	¿Cómo es X?
Teacher:	¿Somos inteligentes?
	americanos
	hispanos
Teacher:	No, no somos hispanos. Somos . . .
Teacher:	¿Estamos en la clase de biología?
Teacher:	No, no estamos . . . , estamos . . .
Teacher:	¿Estamos en la ciudad de México?
Teacher:	No, estamos en . . .
Teacher:	¿Están detrás de A y B (dos estudiantes)?
Teacher:	No, no están detrás de . . .
Teacher:	¿Soy hispano(a)?
Teacher:	No, no soy hispano(a) . . . .

   The preceding is the modeling done by the teacher. The students respond to the first series of questions that are in the affirmative.

Teacher:	¿Estamos en la clase de biología?
	¿Estamos en Chicago?
	¿Somos de la ciudad de México?
Student:	No, no estamos en la clase biología.

   (The sentences in typescript below are written on the board by the students.)

A	B
a. Estamos en la clase de español.	a. No estamos en la clase de biología.

Teacher:	Tú estás delante de X, detrás de X, entre Y y Z. Encima del escritorio, debajo de la mesa, en el suelo.

Student responds.

b. **Estoy sentado delante de X.**   b. **No estoy encima de la mesa.**

Fotos: ¿Quién es? (Señor y Señora Reagan)

Teacher: ¿Son hispanos? ¿Son de la ciudad de México?
¿Están en la Casa Blanca?
¿Son ricos, pobres?

Student responds.

c. **Sr. y Sra. Reagan están en la**   c. **No están en Los Angeles.**
Casa Blanca.

Teacher: ¿Eso es un _____?

Student: No, eso no es un _____; eso es un _____.

muchos objectos

Teacher: ¿Eso es el _____ de _____?

Student responds.

d. **Eso es el libro de Sarita.**   d. **Eso no es el lápiz de X.**

Fotos: ¿Quién es?

Teacher: Ella/él es rico(a), inteligente, bonito(a), grande.

Student responds.

Teacher: Ellos son . . .

Student responds.

e. _____ es _____.   e. **Sra. Dupont no es rica.**

Teacher: ¿Estoy delante de, detrás de, etc.?

Student responds.

f. **Tú estás delante de la clase.**   f. **Tú no eres hispana.**

Read and correct the sentences
Extract the rule:

Teacher: ¿Cuál es la diferencia entre A y B?
afirmativa y negativa ¿cuántos partidos?
¿cuáles palabras?
¿la posición?

a la pizarra: *la negativa*
no + verb

3. Review and practice of the negation (5 minutes)

Teacher: ¿Tú estás parado(a)?
en la casa
en el edificio
estoy delante de/detrás de, etc.
los estudiantes son amables, están en la clase, están sentados,
son latinos.

4. Review and correction of the test (5–10 minutes)

5. Games

Interview: Ask questions of your partner that will elicit negative responses. Write down at least three of these answers. I will collect. (5–10 minutes)

Tic-Tac-Toe (remainder of time)

Divide class in half; ask questions regarding negative, past vocabulary, etc. Student must give a completely correct answer in order to choose a space.

6. Conclusion

Explain homework (at end of lesson plan); go over the model, "HASTA LUEGO"

HOMEWORK EXERCISES TO AUGMENT LESSON

1. Escriban en negativo:

   modelo: Soy de la ciudad de México.

           No soy de la ciudad de México.

   a. Eso es un libro.

   b. Eso es el escritorio de la señora.

   c. Soy Consuelo.

   d. María es grande.

   e. Pablo y Gregorio son americanos.

   f. Tú eres de los Estados Unidos.

   g. Estamos en Londres.

   h. La bolsa de ella está en el suelo.

   i. Estoy sentada adelante de Ricardo.

   j. Ellas son rubias.

   k. Juan y usted, ¿Ustedes son de la ciudad de México?

2. Conteste. Use la forma negativa.

   a. ¿Es usted hispano?

   b. ¿Está la profesora detrás del escritorio?

   c. ¿La clase de español es desde las ocho hasta las nueve?

   d. ¿Estamos en Chicago?

ASSESSING THE STRATEGIC PLANNING OF THE LESSON PLAN

Topic of Lesson: Negation: Review of Vocabulary

Lesson Topic: Negation: Review of Vocabulary   Grade Level: High School

1. INSTRUCTIONAL OBJECTIVES

a. Are the objectives stated operationally and in precise and measurable terms?
Yes __X__ No _____

b. Are the objectives developmentally well chosen? Yes __X__ No _____

Comments: Sound and well-chosen objectives; may be too many for one lesson, but could be paced over 2 or more days if needed.

2. MATERIALS

a. Are the instructional materials appropriate for meeting the objectives?
Yes __X__ No _____

b. Are the instructional materials adequate to provide accommodation to different learning styles? Yes __X__ No _____

Comments: Visual and auditory reinforcement are provided; the lesson accommodates both those who enjoy illustrations and those who deal better with texts.

3. MOTIVATION

a. Are the motivational techniques incorporated into the lesson adequate in terms of generating an interest in the lesson? Yes __X__ No _____

b. Are the motivational techniques incorporated into the lesson adequate in terms of maintaining and sustaining an interest in the lesson? Yes __X__ No _____

Comments: The lesson draws well on students' interests. The idea of being aliens in a foreign country is creative and provocative. Also, the use of praise and teacher response should be instrumental in generating and sustaining interest. Good attention both to slower and enriched learners.

4. PROCEDURE
   a. Are the teacher and learner roles/activities during the lesson clearly outlined and explained? Yes __X__ No _____
   b. Are the activities in the instructional sequence congruent with the lesson's objectives? Yes __X__ No _____
   c. Is the lesson plan logically sequenced? Yes __X__ No _____
   d. Do the activities in the lesson provide for individual differences in learning? Yes __X__ No _____
   e. Do the activities in the lesson represent clear examples of the effective use of learning principles? Yes __X__ No _____

Comments: The activities are very well thought out. The lesson contains a very helpful script with the roles clearly outlined. The lesson is logically sequenced in that it starts out with a review and then leads into new concepts. Attention is given to different types of learners and learning styles; the lesson shows sound application of modeling, reinforcement, appropriate practice, and use of various learning modalities.

5. TIME ESTIMATES
   a. Are the time estimates in the lesson appropriately paced? Yes __X__ No _____
   b. Are the time estimates in the lesson realistic? Yes _____ No _____ (Partially)

Comments: The pacing seems sound but I'm not sure if the time allowed overall is adequate. For the activities (board work, seat interviews, etc.),there may be inadequate time allotted.

6. EVALUATION
   a. Is the evaluation of the lesson appropriate in terms of assessment of completed objectives? Yes _____ No _____ (Partially)
   b. Is the evaluation of the lesson appropriate in terms of assessment of the overall success of the lesson design? Yes __X__ No _____

Comments: The lesson contains good questions to assess overall success of the lesson in terms of student involvement and instructional decisions. However, the lesson does not include an evaluation of the actual objective of learning the negative form.

7. INDEPENDENT WORK AND FOLLOW-UP

   a. If independent work is assigned, does such work provide appropriate practice to reinforce the stated objectives?

     Yes __X__   No _____   Not applicable _____

   b. If follow-up assignments are included, do they enhance the stated goals of the lesson plan?   Yes __X__   No _____   Not applicable _____

Comments: The review and practice planned is appropriate.

_____

_____

_____

ELEMENTARY CURRICULUM UNIT PLAN: THE NEWSPAPER

(Pre-Service Project)

Susie Sugerman

University of California,
Los Angeles
Teacher Education Laboratory

Contents

BACKGROUND

This is an upper elementary unit based on the use of the newspaper. It is interdisciplinary and includes group cooperation as a central goal.

Educational Philosophy

The underlying philosophy for this unit is a synthesis of aspects of the cognitive, behavioristic, and humanistic approaches to education. First, the cognitive approach will be used during the planning, implementation, and evaluation of the unit, taking into account the developmental stage of each learner. Second, for classroom management and the reinforcement of learning, certain behavioristic techniques will be utilized. And finally, all people need to be recognized as individuals of worth; therefore, humanistic tenets will be incorporated into the unit as well.

School and Community

The school for which this unit was designed is a well-integrated school, with the following ethnic and racial groups represented: 46 percent black, 45 percent white, and 7 percent other (Hispanic, Asian, etc.). The socioeconomic status of the students ranges from very low-income to very high-income families. The community is very supportive of the school and its program; the support is reflected in high parental involvement in the school.

Specific Student to Be Taught

The Newspaper Unit has been designed with a specific sixth-grade class in mind. There are thirty-seven students in the class, nineteen girls and seventeen boys. Eighteen students are black, fifteen are white, and three are Asian. There is a broad span of achievement levels in the basic skills; the majority of the students are at or near grade level. Socially, the class is basically cooperative but not entirely cohesive. There is a range of attitudes, from negative to very positive, demonstrated toward school. Individual success and competition seem stronger among the students than team work and mutual support. There are several strong leaders in the group. Every student has a special quality and something to contribute to the group.

UNIT DESCRIPTION

A description of the unit is provided in this section. It includes why the topic was chosen and the objectives of the unit.

Topic and Reasons Selected

The topic for this unit is the newspaper, selected for the reasons which follow. Because the class for which this unit was designed lacked group cohesiveness, I selected a topic which would stimulate the students to work toward a mutual goal. They have responded well to current events and appeared interested in world news. Therefore, I developed this six-week unit to encourage group cooperation and promote academic enrichment in social studies, history, and oral and written communication. The interdisciplinary approach, used in this unit, has proven effective with this grade level. Also, the production of a product, which this unit will yield in the form of a class newspaper, will increase pride and motivation in the lessons.

Goals

- The students will develop an understanding of how the newspaper is produced and the important role it plays in our everyday lives.
- The students will develop an appreciation of working effectively in a group.
- The students will develop oral and written communication skills.

Objectives

By the end of the unit:

- The learner will have composed a notebook containing a specified number of a variety of newspaper clippings read during the first week of the unit.
- The learner will have written an effective news lead utilizing the 5 Ws and 1 H structure.
- The learner will have participated in the writing of a group research report on a famous journalist and presented findings to the class.
- The learner will have written a news story utilizing the correct inverted pyramid structure.
- The learner will have participated in composing a group thank-you note to the local newspaper toured.
- The learner will have written three headlines that comply with the headline rule sheet.
- The learner will have written a letter to the editor at a local newspaper about a community problem.
- The learner will have created a cartoon (either political or comic) suitable for a newspaper.

- Working in small groups, the learner will have chosen a day in history (applicable to the history learned this year) and composed a rough outline of a front page depicting that day.
- With the teacher's assistance, the learner will have participated in creating a class newspaper, bringing together concepts learned throughout the unit.

INSTRUCTIONAL PLAN

The sequence of the unit plan is provided here. Included is a description of the major activities to be presented.

Task Analysis

The students in this class have had minimal contact with the newspaper; when questioned, it was determined that most do not read the newspaper on a regular basis. Those who read it regularly generally only read a particular section, such as the sports section or the comics. Therefore, the newspaper will be introduced as something everyone should read regularly.

Writing samples have been received throughout the school year, yielding a class profile of writing abilities. Reading scores have been determined; all students are able to handle basic comprehension of the daily newspaper.

After the initial introductory lessons on becoming familiar with the newspaper, the unit will progress as follows in this task analysis format of the subsequent lessons:

1. Teaching the news lead.
2. Teaching the news story.
3. Small-group research project on a famous journalist.
4. Field trip to a local newspaper.
5. Creating a newspaper: writing headlines and letters to the editor; creating cartoons; producing a class newspaper.

A table showing the weekly schedule of activities of the unit plan follows.

Major Activities

ACTIVITY 1 *OBJECTIVE:* The learner will compose a notebook containing a variety of newspaper clippings read during the first week of the unit.

This activity will represent a week's work for each student. Three days (one hour per day) will be allotted in class for work completion, although

WEEKLY SCHEDULE OF ACTIVITIES

WEEK	MONDAY	TUESDAY	WEDNESDAY	THURSDAY	FRIDAY
1	Bring in newspaper. Explain unit. Ask children to read newspaper and bring one to class if possible.	Explain notebook project due Friday. Hand out list of topics for children to cut out. Encourage use of learning center.	Check for comprehension "How are you doing?" Discuss local, state, and world news.	Check again for comprehension. Remind class of due date tomorrow! Share articles in class, showing examples of local, state, and world news.	Notebook due! Share projects. Review. Discuss a bit of what is to come.
2	Praise notebooks and return to class. Introduce the importance of "getting the facts." Recite stories to students and ask them to write down 3 facts.	Review "facts." Introduce structure of a news lead. Use same facts, but show how a lead can be written (teacher). Present 5 Ws.	Review news lead structure. Assign class to individually cut out 2 examples of a news lead and bring to class on Friday. Label 5 Ws. For fun—read "Who's on First."	Give kids facts and ask them to write news lead using style learned. Hand out worksheets for practice. Ask children to choose their best one and turn it in tomorrow with cutout leads.	News leads due. Reinforce by reading some good examples. Introduce small-group report/project on a famous journalist. Break into groups.

WEEK	MONDAY	TUESDAY	WEDNESDAY	THURSDAY	FRIDAY
3	Return leads. Begin on inverted pyramid style. Break up into small groups—famous journalists. Forty mins. for discussion and delegation of responsibilities. Report and project due Friday.	Review inverted pyramid (They should have entire news story structure down by the end of the week). Worksheet on order in news stories. Small groups 40 mins. Assignment—cut 3 news stories from paper—due Friday.	Small groups should be rolling. Reports should be started and any presentation ideas underway. 50 mins. in group, teacher offering help.	Final touches on reports and presentations. Remind class that 3 news articles are due with summaries tomorrow. Build anticipation for tomorrow's presentations.	Presentations! Feedback. Remind students about field trip to local newspaper. Review unit so far.
4	Discuss presentations and hand back reports. Introduce how a newspaper works. Show 17-min. film, *The Newspaper Story*. Ask students to think of questions to ask on trip.	Quick refresher on news story style. Assignment—kids will write a news story on their field trip. Discuss proper behavior for field trip. Get students motivated!	Field trip. Discuss upon return to class. Remind the students that story is due Friday.	Further discussion about field trip. Answer questions about news stories.	Stories due. Read some out loud if possible. Introduce headlines. Group thank-you note to local paper.

WEEK	MONDAY	TUESDAY	WEDNESDAY	THURSDAY	FRIDAY
5	Return stories and discuss; continue on headline rules. Pass out rule sheet. Use headlines throughout day to reinforce idea.	More on headlines. Assignment—3 headlines from paper you really like and 3 of your own. You can write a headline for your news story! Excerpt from either *All the President's Men* or *Absence of Malice*.	Introduce letter to the editor. "What bothers you enough to write about it?" Class discussion.	Time to write letter in class. Review anything students need to know. Introduce class newspaper idea.	Headlines due. Letters due. Read some in class. Introduce cartoons.
6	Work on cartoons/comic strips. Cut out 3 examples and turn in Wednesday with a few lines explaining what each means. For class newspaper, turn in 2 examples of your best work. Due Friday.	Continue cartoons. Due tomorrow. Remind kids about Friday. Encourage to submit group reports, cartoons, and leads. Decide if paper will be put together by staff, teacher, etc.	Cartoons due. Discussion of the unit. What have you learned? Questionnaires about unit. What would they change? Small groups —pretend you have your own paper. Give history dates. Discuss.	More small groups. Assignment—in group, make a layout of front page. Hand out rule sheet. What is your paper's name? Presentation tomorrow.	Presentations of newspaper names and front page in history. Collect articles. Review questionnaires. Announcements about class newspaper.

homework will be encouraged. This notebook is a motivational technique to promote students' appreciation of the newspaper. The notebook can be self-made or bought; this is entirely up to the individual. An emphasis on pride in this notebook will be promoted *this* week especially, and will carry over to the following weeks, when the children will add other items (news leads, headlines, etc.) to the notebook. The instructional strategy is lecture at the outset when I explain the project. The actual completion of the task, however, is individualized.

ACTIVITY 2 *OBJECTIVE:* The learner will write an effective news lead utilizing the 5 Ws and 1 H structure.

This activity is preceded by a class lecture on fact finding. When the students have mastered that concept, they will be ready to understand and eventually write effective news leads. This activity will occupy a rather substantial length of time (one and a half weeks, one hour per day) because comprehension of the concept is crucial to the understanding of the entire news story structure. The instructional modes will be both lecture and kinesthetic as evidenced by the lesson plan provided. Practice throughout the seven days will manifest itself in worksheets, review, and reinforcing lectures. (A sample lesson plan for this activity follows Activity 9.)

ACTIVITY 3 *OBJECTIVE:* The learner will participate in the writing of a group research paper on a famous journalist and will be responsible for participating in some kind of presentation findings to the class.

This group activity relates to the unit goal of having the students work effectively in groups. I will give little instruction in an effort to have them rely on one other for solutions to their problems. They will have a little more than a week (about forty-five minutes each day) to formulate ideas and to research (either at the school library or a local one), write, and present the report. I will emphasize creativity in their ten-minute presentations. For example, they can present their information in a group play, a poem, or a newscast. This activity draws from many content areas, including English, history, and drama, and will provide learning and entertainment simultaneously.

ACTIVITY 4 *OBJECTIVE:* The learner will write a news story about the trip to the local newspaper, utilizing the correct inverted pyramid structure.

This activity is a culmination of a few prior activities: mastery of the news lead, film and discussion about how the newspaper works prior to the field trip to the local paper, and the field trip itself. We will refresh our memories about proper news story structure, discuss a film entitled *The Newspaper Story,* and contemplate and evaluate the field trip. After a week of such learning, the child should be able to write a clear, concise story about the half-day field trip (who was met, what was seen, etc.). A follow-up exercise will be a group thank-you note to the newspaper in care of our tour guide.

ACTIVITY 5 *OBJECTIVE:* The learner will write three headlines that comply with the headline rule sheet.

Instruction will last about three days (approximately one hour each day) on this subject. Basic rules will be taught and meaningful examples given. The students will gain further understanding of the concept by finding headlines in the newspaper and adding them to their clipping notebooks. I will reinforce the idea of headlines by writing directions on the board in headline style and occasionally speaking in headline format while teaching other subjects in the school day. The headlines generated by students will be included in a newspaper bulletin board, posted at the learning center or returned to the students.

ACTIVITY 6 *OBJECTIVE:*   The learner will write a letter to the editor of a local newspaper about a community problem voted on by the class.

We will decide as a class on a problem that concerns all of us. Then individually the children will write a letter to the editor explaining their views and providing a solution to the problem. For example, we might address the issue of establishing no-smoking sections in public places. This will be a two-day assignment (one hour both days), and time will be given in class to compose the letter. I will copy each letter and send the packet to a local paper (maybe the one we visited) and encourage the children to see if any are published. This activity is designed to improve group interaction as well as develop a social conscience and concern for community problems. If necessary, parental consent forms will be sent home to approve the sending of the letters to the paper.

ACTIVITY 7 *OBJECTIVE:*   The learner will create a cartoon (either political or comic) suitable for a newspaper.

This activity serves to bring art into our newspaper unit. Again, finding three examples of cartoons in the newspaper will reinforce the cartoon concept. The children will have four days (about forty-five minutes each day) to complete their cartoons, and all of the children will have the opportunity to share their cartoons with the class. In my instructions, I will show examples and ask the students for possible cartoon topics. The finished cartoons will either go on the bulletin board, at the learning center, or in the clipping notebook.

ACTIVITY 8 *OBJECTIVE:*   Working in small groups, the learner will choose a date in history (applicable to the history learned during the year) and compose a rough outline of a front page depicting that day.

A guideline sheet will accompany this activity giving the following rules: The paper must have a name, at least one cartoon, and at least four stories with headlines. The children will present their papers to the class explaining the main points (lead) of each story. This group effort will be predominantly up to the students, but this would be optional. This activity will occupy three days (one hour each day), providing time to do any research at the library that is needed.

ELEMENTARY LESSON PLAN

Lesson Topic: _____Writing a News Lead_____

Unit Topic: _____The Newspaper_____ Grade Level: ____6____

1. INSTRUCTIONAL OBJECTIVE
The learner will write an effective news lead utilizing the five Ws and 1 H structure.

2. MATERIALS
8½ x 11 papers labeled *Who, What, When, Where, Why,* and *How,* to be used to emphasize the usage of these question words in a news lead.

3. MOTIVATION
Who can tell me what a line leader does? We call the first paragraph in a news story a news lead for the very same reason. A news lead leads us into the story just as a line leader leads us into the room. The lead helps us to know where we are going. It contains the most important information of the story all in one sentence! It should also capture your attention so you want to read the rest of the story. Today we will learn about how to write a news lead [this lesson will actually take two days]. Here's an example [uncover following paragraph written ahead on board]:

"Room 13 eagerly learned how to write a news lead today in their classroom when their teacher told them it was an important concept to understand in their newspaper unit."

4. PROCEDURE
Who would like to read this out loud? Joey . . . Everyone should be reading along with Joey because I will be asking some important questions after he is through. Five of my questions begin with W. If you answer correctly you will receive one of these cards [hand out as children respond].

    a. *Who* learned something? Underline answer in example.
    b. *What* did they learn?
    c. *When* did they learn?
    d. *Where* did they learn?
    e. *Why* did they learn?

My last question does not begin with a W and it applies to a later example. Just remember the question *How?*

Now, when I say a part of this lead, I'd like the person holding that W to come up to the front.

    a. Today
    b. Room 13, etc.

Good! Let's say these five Ws together . . . [say words in unison]. Remember, they are all words that begin a question. Don't forget about poor old *How* [hold up]. We'll meet him later! A proper news lead should answer every question.

Here's another example [uncover]:

"On November 15, 1986, a boy from Carthay Center School ate seven hot fudge sundaes at the corner ice cream store in an effort to break the school record."

Mary—you were *Who* last time. Please ask your question word to the class and then ask someone to answer it. If the student is correct, give her/him your card. The whole class should be thinking . . . [proceed through all cards].

Let's try one more [uncover]:

"The UCLA Bruins beat the USC Trojans 27 to 17 last Saturday at the Coliseum by scoring 21 points in the second half of the game."

When I say a part of the sentence, I would like you to raise one finger if it is a *Who* answer, two fingers if it is a *What* answer, etc.

[The cards will be up in front facing the students in numerical order. If most of the students can distinguish the answers, move on to independent work.]

5. TIME ESTIMATES

Motivation—5 minutes

Procedure—25 minutes for the first day. If a second day is necessary to ensure comprehension, 20 minutes should be allotted.

Independent Work—20 minutes.

6. EVALUATION

Was I clear and concise in the explanation of news leads? Did I give examples the students found interesting? Did the students seem motivated? Could they keep up with me and the concepts I was giving them? Did the students write leads that adhered to the structure I taught them?

7. INDEPENDENT WORK AND FOLLOW-UP

Hand out worksheet entitled "Follow the Lead!" (at end of lesson plan). Go over first example with the students and then walk around answering questions. Assign unfinished work for homework and add one more original lead to their assignment. Explain that we will review tomorrow (thus the two-day lesson) and that we will have more practice. Lower their level of concern! This might be a difficult concept.

Follow-up: Review concepts throughout the next week and one half. Use enrichment worksheets and incorporate upcoming unit topic of news stories.

FOLLOW THE LEAD!

Label the facts in numbers 1 and 2 below *Who, What, When, Where, Why,* and *How.* The problems may *not* contain an example of all six possible question words. After you have labeled them, write a news lead using the facts. Remember—be informative *and* exciting! For number 3, write your own set of facts and an original news lead using them.

1. a. He was invited by the school to discuss crime
   b. A policeman
   c. Yesterday
   d. In the auditorium
   e. To talk to sixth-graders

2. a. Last week
   b. Voted
   c. 100 sixth-graders
   d. In the cafeteria
   e. In order to support the candidates

3. Write your own news lead. Write down your facts first, label them, and then write your lead. This is your chance to *lead* your way to becoming a famous journalist. Good luck!

_____

_____

_____

_____

_____

_____

_____

_____

ACTIVITY 9 *OBJECTIVE:*   With the teacher's assistance, the learner will participate in the creation of a class newspaper, bringing together concepts learned throughout the unit.

The students will turn in two of their best writings and/or cartoons completed during the unit and submit them to the editor (the teacher). I will type some up in columns and help the students lay out the pages. I will then process the newspaper and distribute it the following week. How much the children are involved here depends on their interest level. If the level is high we could make a project out of creating a newspaper, selecting a name for the paper, a theme, etc. The main objective I would like to accomplish here is to put as much of the children's work in the paper as possible—to give them something they can be proud of!

RESOURCES AND INSTRUCTIONAL MATERIALS

The resources used in the design of this unit are included here with ideas for extending the underlying concepts and objectives. Sample worksheets are also included.

Student Materials and Texts

1. Reporter's pad and pencil
2. Books (These books are not used as textbooks, but they are used for enrichment at learning centers or during independent work.)
   a. *Junior High Journalism* by Homer L. Hall
   b. *Headlines and Deadlines* by April Koral
   c. *The Newspaper: Its Place in a Democracy* by Duane Bradley
3. Worksheets
   a. "Know Your Newspaper"
   b. "Get the Facts"—A worksheet asking the child to write down five important facts from a story written on the sheet
   c. "Follow the Lead"—Contains important information on news leads and practice exercises on how to write an effective lead
   d. "Famous Journalists"—A list is provided of ten famous journalists, for the teacher's use, mainly, although students may wish to research some of these individuals on their own
   e. "I'm So Confused—Put Me in Order!" Practice in putting paragraphs in the inverted pyramid style in news stories. Cut out paragraphs on an article in a newspaper and ask children to put it together. Can be a worksheet or actual news story to be worked on in groups.
   f. "Headline Rules"—List of rules about headlines. How technical the rules become depends on level and progress of the class.
4. Use of local newspapers that have education departments

KNOW YOUR NEWSPAPER!

A newspaper is a tremendous source all types of news, ideas, and interesting information. Your assignment is to get acquainted with newspapers by discovering the different features a newspaper contains.

Below is a list of new topics. You are to find an article on *each* topic. Glue, tape, or staple each clipping neatly onto a piece of paper, labeling each page. Make your own notebook or purchase one; it's up to you. Your newspaper notebook is something to be proud of!

1. World news
2. National news
3. State news
4. Local news
5. Editorials (opinions)
6. Sports
7. Weather
8. Comics (comic strips)
9. Political cartoon
10. Classified ads
11. Financial news—the stock market
12. Movie reviews
13. Letters-to-the-editor
14. ''Dear Abby'' letter
15. Anything else you would like to add

Have fun getting to know your newspaper! You'll be glad you did!

GET THE FACTS!

Write down *five* important facts from this story. Many facts are important, but you may only choose FIVE!

"Friends of Carthay," a parent volunteer group, put on a Halloween Breakfast October 30, 1983, on the playground, in order to raise money for the school.

Pancakes, sausage, and orange juice were served by the parents. In addition to the food sale, there was a haunted house and a sweatshirt booth where everyone could buy sweatshirts.

Many children dressed up in their Halloween costumes, and it seemed like fun was had by all.

Fact 1 _____

Fact 2 _____

Fact 3 _____

Fact 4 _____

Fact 5 _____

FAMOUS JOURNALISTS

For Group Work and Learning Center

1. John Peter Zenger—*New York Weekly Journal* 1733 "Free Press"
2. Benjamin Harris—First American newspaper
3. Benjamin H. Day—Penny newspaper
4. Horace Greeley—*New York Tribune*
5. William Randolph Hearst—Sensationalism
6. Joseph Pulitzer—Sensationalism
7. Edward Wyllis Scripps—First chain newspaper
8. Benjamin Franklin
9. Walter Lippman
10. William F. Buckley, Jr.

This is a teacher's aid. Names of the six most interesting and easily researched journalists will be assigned to group work, while the other journalists will appear in the learning center.

Audiovisual Resources, Field Trips

1. Film: *The Newspaper Story*—Steps outlined and explained in the completion of a news story from recording the incident, taking pictures, writing, editing, setting type, printing, and distributing
2. Field trip to a local newspaper
3. Excerpts (if possible and allowable) of:
   a. *All the President's Men*
   b. *Absence of Malice*

Additional Ideas

1. *Bulletin Boards:* Each board will be up for two weeks during the unit.
   Sample Displays:

2. *Learning Centers:* Title—"We Have Noses for News"
   Week 1 Newspapers to read. Purpose: exposure to the newspaper.
   Week 2 Listen to a fast-breaking story on a tape recorder. Write down three important facts and put in a box attached to the center with your name on it.
   Week 3 Choose a card with facts. Write a news lead using the same structure we learned in class.
   Week 4 Meet a famous journalist. Choose a card with facts about a journalist. Write a story about the person you met.
   Week 5 *Headlines and Deadlines*—A book ideally suited for reinforcement of the field trip to the local newspaper. The book is filled with vivid pictures and excellent text regarding how a newspaper is made. In addition, a worksheet entitled "Headline Hunting" will be available.
   Week 6 Put a puzzle together of a front-page layout.

BIBLIOGRAPHIES

Resources

1. Primarily my own knowledge of the newspaper and field of journalism
2. Media Resource Center—UCLA
   The Newspaper Story—4195; 17 minutes long
3. Bradley, Duane. *The Newspaper: Its Place in a Democracy.* Princeton:
   D. Van Nostrand Company, Inc., 1965.
   Hall, Homer L. *Junior High Journalism.* New York: Richards Rosen Press,
   1969.
   Koral, April. *Headlines and Deadlines.* New York: Julian Messner, 1981.

Students' Resources—Bibliography

1. Same books for learning centers and enrichment study.
2. Worksheets, learning centers, and bulletin boards are my own ideas for
   the most part. The NOTEBOOK worksheet was derived by Ida Rodich,
   my master teacher. I adapted the sheet from her original idea.

Added resources from *Bartlett's Book of Quotations*

1. "All the news that's fit to print."
   —Motto of *N.Y. Times*
2. "When a dog bites a man that is not news because it happens so often.
   But if a man bites a dog, that is news."
   —From Frank M. O'Brien
3. "This news is old enough but it is every day's news."
   —William Shakespeare
4. "The vital measure of a newspaper is not its size but its spirit—that is its
   responsibility to report the news fully, accurately and fairly."
   —Arthur Hays Sulzberger

These will be written on the blackboard throughout the unit.

EVALUATION PROCEDURES

This section contains the essential steps taken in evaluating students before,
during, and at the end of instruction. Sample forms and questions are included where appropriate.

1. Preassessment Chart

This chart will plot students' abilities in each specified category prior to implementing the unit.

NAME	INTEREST LEVEL weeks 1&2 3&4 5&6			WRITING SAMPLES weeks 1&2 3&4 5&6			GROUP COOPERATION weeks 1&2 3&4 5&6			GETS WORK IN ON TIME weeks 1&2 3&4 5&6		
Alex												
Gita												
Geoff												
Susan												
Lupe												

A grade sheet should be attached for each student containing graded projects and observations made about each student's progress throughout the unit.

2. Assessing Student Interest Level

Distribute the following questionnaire to students prior to the unit:

a. Do you receive the newspaper at your home?
b. If yes, do you read it? If you do not receive it, do you ever see any one else's newspaper? Whose?
c. What sections do you read?
d. Write three items that are "in the news" at this time.
e. What would you like to learn about the newspaper?

Rank each child one to ten according to answers. Write ten in the first column if the child shows a high degree of interest and/or knowledge, five if somewhere in the middle, etc. All other categories will follow this same structure—one being the lowest score and ten being the highest. By the end of the unit, three scores will appear in each category and improvement can be noted.

3. Writing Samples

I plan to begin this unit in the middle of the year, when I have sufficient examples of the students' writing abilities. I will especially look for clear expression of ideas and use of sound structure because good newspaper writing requires these skills. Other writing skills essential to this unit are knowledge of appropriate sentence structure (avoiding run-ons), of when to make a new paragraph, and of basic grammatical rules. Again, the students will be rated one to ten.

4. Assessing Group Cooperation

This assessment is done through observation. I will look for a child's ability to get along well with others, to add constructive comments in a group, to assume leadership or to accept leadership skills in others, and to both respect and gain the respect of peers. From the rankings in this category, I will determine groupings for small-group projects, mixing students who work well in groups with those who do not.

5. Ability to Turn in Assignments on Time

This assessment will also be a survey of the students' performance throughout the year. The unit's success is partly determined by the students' ability to follow the schedule set up for them. Each activity relates to the preceding one. Feedback on that past activity is necessary if the student is to excel on the next activity.

Note About Grouping

Although there is a great difference between high and low academic levels of students in my class, I did not plan for grouped remedial instruction. To any children with problems I will offer extra personal attention and reinforcement worksheets. The students requiring added stimuli can work at the learning centers; in addition, they can help their peers who are having difficulty with certain concepts. None of the activities should present too much of a problem because each child can always perform at his or her own level. The group activities will be divided into students varying in ranges of ability. This heterogeneous grouping should develop leadership skills in the high achieving children and should push the slower children to keep up.

Formative Evaluation

Activities	Assignments and Assessments
1. Notebook Project	Assign Tuesday. Review and take questions Wednesday. Share examples in class Thursday. Notebook due Friday. Review books, make comments, and turn back Monday. Graded assignment A–F.
2. News Leads	Introduce Tuesday (worksheet). Review Wednesday. Worksheet Thursday (similar to that on Tuesday). Due Friday. Assess progress by effectiveness of leads. Grade and return with comments Monday.

Activities	Assignments and Assessments
3. Group Research Project: Famous Journalist	Assign Friday and discuss. Monday—small-group work. Teacher should roam around. Continue same format Wednesday and Thursday. Answer any questions. Assess by observation and class discussion how everything is going. Friday—presentations and feedback by teacher. Group grade.
4. News Story on Field Trip	*Monday*—film on the making of a news story. Discussion will provide assessment. *Tuesday*—worksheet on news story structure (mixed-up paragraphs are put in correct order). Assignment given. *Wednesday*—field trip and review of the day. Discuss how the day's events apply to assignment. *Thursday*—examples of news stories distributed and discussed. *Friday*—due date. Review and turn back.
5. Headlines	*Friday*—introduce headlines through lecture. *Monday*—distribute rule sheets. Discuss rule sheets and write samples as a class. *Tuesday*—announce assignment due. *Friday*—review. *Friday*—assess progress and return work graded on Monday.
6. Letter-to-Editor	*Wednesday*—introduce idea through lecture and discussion. Assess knowledge of subject by choice of community problem. Assignment due Friday. *Thursday*—time in class to do work. Teacher roams around to check progress and answer any problems. Assess on Friday and return to students on *Monday*—graded.
7. Cartoon	*Friday*—introduce using lecture and examples. Monday and Tuesday allow time to work in class. Observe activity and advise. *Wednesday*—cartoons due. Assess and return graded.
8. Small Group: A Day in History	Group work Tuesday, Wednesday, Thursday. Be available for questions and be ready to provide clues as to where to research, ideas for days, etc.

Activities	Assignments and Assessments
	Friday—presentations. Group grade. Assess students' creativity and enthusiasm.
9. Class Newspaper	Open-ended, determined by student interest and progress during the unit.

The assessments outlined for formative evaluation are positioned at times when the students have had sufficient time to adequately master the concept. Due dates are always on Friday (except for the cartoons), so that the children have a good idea of what is expected and when. Because of the structure and rather fast pace of the unit, the assessment dates are quite stringent. The quick return of all assignments back to the children will model desired behavior of getting work in and out promptly.

All in all, learning will be assessed by performance on assignments, and worksheets and in group interaction. The type of assessments to be used are:

1. *Observation*—used especially with affective goal of working together. Children's behavior should constantly be observed to note progress.

2. *Written assignments*—various assignments specified throughout the unit will be assessed and graded.

3. *Group discussion*—this assessment technique should be used when the time feels right. Effective for reviewing material and giving feedback on progress.

4. *Group presentations*—another way of checking for understanding. Do the students seem motivated and clear on the topic of their presentation? Also important when assessing group cooperation.

Unit Evaluation

1. Questions about content:
   a. Was pace too fast; too short? Or okay?
   b. Did content interest students? Were they excited to begin each day with the newspaper unit?
   c. Did the assignments make the students feel overloaded with work?
   d. Was the topic presented in such a way that the students could apply their knowledge to their daily lives?
   e. Did the students improve their group cooperation skills throughout the unit? Were enough group activities included to teach the concept?
   f. Did the students show an understanding of a majority of the assignments? Were they ever confused; frustrated?

2. Questions for teacher evaluation:
   a. Did I make the subject come alive for the students?
   b. Was there a varied amount of teaching strategies (group, lecture, individualized)?
   c. Did I wait to move on until the students had a handle on a certain concept, or did I rush ahead to be on cue with my lesson planning?

    d. Did I make myself available enough to answer individual questions and help with any problems that arose?

    e. Did I direct students to resources where they could further their knowledge on newspapers?

    f. Did I adequately and effectively model and reinforce getting along with others?

    g. Did I grade fairly, accurately? Did I give the students enough verbal and written feedback in a timely manner?

3. Student feedback

    The questionnaire which follows will be handed out to students during the sixth week of the unit. Discussion of the results would follow the next day.

Evaluation of Newspaper Unit

Circle yes or no on the first five questions.

1. I am more interested in the newspaper today than I was six weeks ago.   yes no

2. I want to learn even more about the newspaper.   yes no

3. I feel I can work well in a group.   yes no

4. I'm glad we went on the field trip.   yes no

5. I have shared what I learned with my family/friends.   yes no

Please answer the following questions. They will be very helpful to me in determining the success of this newspaper unit. Feel free to use the back side of this paper for your replies.

1. What was your favorite part of this unit? Why?

2. What was your least favorite part of this unit? Why?

3. What would you change for students who have this unit next year? Be specific!

4. What do you wish the teacher had done differently? How would *you* have done it?

5. Anything else you wish to add?

ASSESSING THE STRATEGIC PLANNING OF THE TEACHING UNIT

Unit Topic: ___The Newspaper___   Grade Level: ___6___

1. BACKGROUND INFORMATION

   a. Is the background information provided adequate in conveying the underlying philosophy of the unit? Yes __X__ No _____

   b. Does the background information provide a concise profile of the learners? Yes __X__ No _____

Comments: The background information, although brief, provides the reader with a general philosophical and educational framework within which to assess the unit.

2. UNIT DESCRIPTION

   a. Does the unit description offer a clear explanation of the rationale for implementing the unit? Yes __X__ No _____

   b. Are the goals and objectives of the unit:
   • Clearly stated? Yes __X__ No _____
   • Comprehensive enough to support the planned scope of the unit? Yes __X__ No _____

Comments: The goals are broad and comprehensive. Generally, the objectives seem comprehensive in supporting the interdisciplinary approach. Certain objectives might be more precisely stated, i.e., objectives containing "participate"; may be helpful to give exact behaviors learners will demonstrate within those activities.

3. INSTRUCTIONAL PLAN:

   a. Task Analysis—Is the task analysis complete in providing:
   • A clear and sound assessment of entry-level behavior? Yes _____ No __X__ (See Comments)
   • Appropriate and comprehensive intermediate steps? Yes _____ No __X__ (See Comments)
   • A complete set of target behaviors which match the instructional objectives? Yes _____ No __X__ (See Comments)

b. Activities—Are the scheduled activities:
- Sufficiently comprehensive to achieve the planned objectives?
Yes __X__ No _____
- Presented in a logical sequence so as to maximize the achievement of the objective? Yes __X__ No _____
- Clearly stated with sufficient amplification to provide a clear instructional picture of their intent? Yes __X__ No _____

c. Sample Daily Lesson Plans—Does the sample daily lesson plan:
- Model a sound and comprehensive lesson plan? Yes __X__ No _____
- Lead to the mastery of the stated objectives? Yes __X__ No _____

Comments: The task analysis appears to be the only weak section of this paper in that it is incomplete. (1) What are the prerequisite skills and knowledge needed before the learner can perform in accordance with the objectives? (list them.) (2) Which of the prerequisites will be taught in the learning activities, and which will be considered "entry behaviors" (requirements that the learner is expected to demonstrate on entrance to the learning activity)? The first paragraph under "Task Analysis" seems better suited for under "Topic of Unit and Response Selected."

The activities are sound and comprehensive in scope. They are well paced to ensure review and appropriate practice time. In the "Schedule of Activities by Weeks," we believe it would have been helpful to refer to the worksheets by their titles.

Overall the lesson plan is solid and well thought-out. It is based on the learning principles of motivation (personal lives of students, participation in "game" with cards, etc.) and in most cases appropriate practice. However the class needs to be given practice in writing original leads before being given independent worksheets calling for this behavior.

4. RESOURCES AND INSTRUCTIONAL MATERIALS:

Are the resources and instructional materials used in the unit:
- Comprehensive enough to support the unit? Yes __X__ No _____
- Oriented toward a variety of learning styles? Yes __X__ No _____

Comments: The worksheets are well formulated and suited to the objectives. They provide usual (bulletin boards, board work), auditory (listening centers), and kinesthetic (working with flash-card games) stimuli for the learners. We would suggest adding some additional resources and/or information so that other teachers (besides the author) could use the unit. First, the headline rules need to be given. Second, an explication of the inverted pyramid structure is desirable. Students should at least be told where they can find such information. Two excellent resources include: Cheyney, Arnold B. The Writing Corner. Glenview, IL: Scott, Foresman and Company, 1979; and Shrot, J. Rodney, and Dickerson, Bev. The Newspaper: An Alternative Textbook. Belmont, CA; Pitman Learning, Inc., 1980. The reader may also need more information on precisely how the excerpts of All the Presidents' Men and Absence of Malice are to be used. Which excerpts are best suited for the purpose of this unit?

5. EVALUATION PROCEDURES:

a. Preassessment—Is the preassessment planned for the unit:
- Appropriate for the learners? Yes __X__ No _____
- Adequate for the planned objectives? Yes _____ No _____ (Partially)

b. Formative Evaluation—Are the criterion checks adequate enough to ensure ongoing successful mastery of the unit objectives? Yes __X__ No _____

c. Unit Evaluation—Does the unit evaluation:
- Include all target instructional objectives?
  Yes _____ No __X__ (*See Comments)
- Provide for adequate teacher and student input? Yes __X__ No _____

Comments: Thorough and appropriate preassessment to support many goal areas of unit (student interest, group cooperation, and getting work in on time). However specific writing skills (ability to write a news lead, ability to write a leadline, etc.) need to be pretested. A general rating of writing samples seems too broad for the planned objectives.

*Again specific writing skills should be included in the unit evaluation.

The format of the preassessment chart may be confusing. The picture chart is a unit progress chart, not a preassessment chart, but this fact is not apparent at first glance. We suggest combining the two charts. A "preassessment" column could be added to the left of each "weeks 1 and 2" column. Also specific writing skills could serve as headings to replace the "Writing Samples" heading.

If a general rating of writing samples is retained, at least specify all the elements one is considering when making the rating of overall writing quality. (Some abilities are given in the Evaluation section, item III, Writing Samples. Are there others?)

SECONDARY CURRICULUM UNIT PLAN: THE FIRST FIVE WEEKS OF SPANISH I OR FRENCH I

(Pre-Service Project)

Dina Passi
Julie T. Branica
University of California,
Los Angeles
Teacher Education Laboratory

Contents

BACKGROUND

This is a secondary unit plan for the teaching of a foreign language. Cultural and geographical aspects of the target country are included as part of the content.

Educational Philosophy

The art of teaching is the art of guiding, of leading the students to a goal. It is not a process of dictating ideas or behavior. Teaching is presenting facts and material to the students and allowing them to draw conclusions. Ideally, teacher and student form a cohesive unit working toward a common goal, namely, the comprehension of concepts or the successful acquisition of skills. These skills, such as skills of communication, observation, deduction, analysis, and synthesis, should not be narrowly based but adaptable and transferable to real life.

Learning should involve all of the senses and should include all cognitive stages indicated in Bloom's Taxonomy. The more complete the involvement of the learner, the more extensive and meaningful the learning will be. Therefore, the teacher should attempt to incorporate the cognitive, affective, and psychomotor areas of learning into the classroom environment.

In its structural conceptualization and its applied activities and lessons, this unit attempts to incorporate the tenets just outlined.

School and Community

The school in which this unit will be implemented is a predominantly middle-class school, with the following ethnic percentages reflected in the student body: 40 percent Hispanic, 25 percent black, 20 percent Asian, and 15 percent white. The majority of the students (approximately 55 percent) are from middle-income families, approximately 40 percent come from low-income families, and approximately 5 percent from upper-class homes. The importance of the ethnic variety represented in the student body is reflected in the design and selection of this particular unit. Cultural awareness and acceptance, for example, the acquisition of a second language, are primary goals in the school.

Specific Students to Be Taught

The unit is designed for high school students; a potential class could be made up of all grade levels represented in the school. The specific class for which this unit is intended comprises twenty-five tenth and eleventh-grade students —60 percent females, 50 percent nonnative English speakers, and 40 percent university bound. The percentages of ethnic groups—40 percent Hispanic, 35 percent black, 20 percent Asian, and 5 percent white—reflect the basic ethnic breakdown of the student body population.

In terms of social interaction, class members are quite cooperative with the teacher and with one other; their self-esteem is rated quite high. In terms of creativity, they are above average but could use more opportunities to develop their individual gifts. There are a few key leaders in the group. Attitude toward school is mixed, showing a wide range, from very negative to very positive.

UNIT DESCRIPTION

Topic and Reasons Selected

This is a foreign language unit applicable for beginning French or Spanish courses.

The following conceptual framework for the unit will be explained to the students. It will be created and set during the initial lessons, and it will continue throughout the course.

The target language and country will be perceived as an unknown territory that the students (who will be identified as spies or aliens) will discover and explore with the aid of the teacher (who will serve as a guide who has previously visited the country).

The group has been sent to the target city. Our goal is to learn as much as we can in a one-year time frame so that we can convey this information to our leaders and countrymen/women.

Since we have been left in the target country during tourist off-season, we will be forced to communicate with the inhabitants (teacher, other students) in the target language. Of course, we will first learn the words and phrases most frequently heard and used so that we may communicate with the natives. We will learn as much as we can as quickly as possible so that the natives do not realize that they are being observed by foreign beings.

The introduction to and situating of the target country will simulate a process most likely to occur if we were to approach the target area by spaceship. This will be done via maps.

The students will observe and analyze (1) maps of the world and of Europe or Central/South America, (2) a geographical map of the target country, (3) a large street map of the target city, and (4) views inside the city, which can be photos, slides, posters, etc. At the same time, we will play a tape of sounds one would hear in the city: horns, people talking, etc. Several basic expressions *(bonjour, Buenos dias)* will dominate the tape recording.

At the end of each phase or after the complete cycle, the teacher will ask the students to mention whatever they noticed at each step. For example, France is bordered by Spain, Italy, . . .; names of rivers, mountain ranges, specific words or sounds they heard. The teacher will guide and label these observations.

The students will be told to record this information in a log book that they will eventually return to their leader. Each week there will be one-half hour to one full hour follow-up lesson on the culture of the target country. This will include such information as history, food, music, mores, schooling, politics, etc. The teacher will also have the option of incorporating the lesson on culture into the lesson on grammar.

Books, magazines, newspapers, television programs, and films will be regarded as the tools of our discovery process. Later in the year, students will be required to give a presentation of their observations.

This theme was selected because it lends itself to a direct method of foreign language teaching. It allows us to avoid the constant use of English, which often acts as a block to the learning process. The theme of discovery will appeal to the students' sense of curiosity. We selected this theme because it can also be perceived as a sort of game; the elements are presented to the students, who must decode them and then find the logic or patterns behind the connections. It is very much like a puzzle. The theme depends on and encourages the development of the students' skills of logic, analysis, synthesis, and communication.

Not only does the theme allow learning that incorporates all the senses—sight, hearing, touch, smell, and taste—but it is also the most effective way to stimulate confluent learning and convergent and divergent thinking.

By using this theme, we intend to encourage the study of both the language and the culture of the target country. We want to teach students more than words or phrases. We want to present them with a more global view of the target country. Often, foreign language study is not stimulating because the classes concentrate on one aspect of the language, namely the grammar. In many courses, the other facets of the language, including the culture that shaped it and that was shaped by it, are never explored. We want students to see that a language is more than words strung together.

Objectives

The skill objectives and the content we plan to include are categorized under four major groups: the acquisition of idiomatic sentences and/or expressions, language pronunciation, the grammar, and the culture.

Idiomatic sentences.   During class the learners will refer to a given list of idiomatic expressions and choose the appropriate one to indicate their needs to the teacher (e.g., to ask the teacher to repeat, to let the teacher know that they don't understand, or to ask the teacher how to say something or how to write something in the target language).

Pronunciation.   The learner will:
- recite the vowels in the target language with the correct pronunciation.
- recite the alphabet with the correct pronunciation.
- identify those letters which are different from those in the learner's native language and use them correctly.
- recognize the various sounds of the target language and pronounce them correctly when reading aloud.
- identify the sound with the correct symbol and write it correctly when taking dictation at the blackboard or on paper.
- use the correct spelling in the target language to represent the designated sounds.
- use proper stress when appropriate.
- indicate whether a word needs orthographic accent or not, according to the pronunciation given by the teacher.
- use the accepted abbreviations used in the target language and pronounce the word for which these abbreviations stand.
- use correct capitalization in the target language (e.g., for months, days of the week) and when applicable, identify this as a difference between the native language and the target language.

Grammar.   The learner will:
- differentiate a masculine noun from a feminine one by looking at the final vowel.
- recognize at least three exceptions to the masculine/feminine rule, illustrate with examples, and explicate why they are considered exceptions.
- conjugate the irregular verb "to be" in singular and in plural, using the correct person and identifying the second person formal.
- demonstrate knowledge that in Spain the second person plural is used but that is not so in the New World.
- place the adjectives in the proper position in relation to the noun and apply the rules of agreement in number and gender when appropriate.
- distinguish between information questions and yes/no questions and formulate them correctly using the proper structure.
- correctly formulate negative structures.
- generate original sentences using newly introduced vocabulary.
- identify the root and the ending of a verb in the infinitive.
- recognize the various endings associated with the different persons of regular -AR verbs.
- apply the endings of the -AR regular verbs and conjugate new regular -AR verbs not presented in class.

- answer correctly when asked what time it is and use the idiomatic expressions that apply.
- describe weather conditions using the appropriate idiomatic expressions.
- recite the days of the week, the months of the year, and the seasons.
- incorporate weather expressions to describe or refer to the months and/or seasons.
- point out that the seasons correspond to the opposite months in the southern hemisphere and apply this fact accordingly.
- formulate questions and give answers which demonstrate that the learner differentiates between *date* and *day*.
- identify at least three different uses of "to be" in the target language (e.g., to express nationality, description: physical and mental, profession, place of origin, etc.).
- use appropriate greeting according to the time of day.
- establish family relationships among three generations (i.e., grandparents, parents, children) in terms of who is father or husband of whom and who is mother or wife of whom.
- recognize the different types of interrogative words and indicate what type of information they request.
- formulate at least three possible questions from a given sentence, using interrogative words (e.g., "Mary goes to the beach every Sunday": Who? Where? When?).
- differentiate between *name* and *surname* formulating the correct question or giving the correct answer.

Culture.   This contains four sections related to four discussion areas. For the target country, the learner will:
- locate correctly on a map of the world at least three countries where the target language is spoken.
- locate correctly on a map of the world at least one country in Europe and one in the New World where the target language is spoken.
- point out on a map of the target country three geographical features that characterize it and give the names (e.g., Seine River, which goes through Paris; Pyrenees Mountain Range on the border of Spain).
- locate correctly on a map of the target country the capital and give its name.
- name at least two major cities of the target country besides the capital.
- correctly match, from a list of twelve, at least seven geographical items with their corresponding description (e.g., Paris—capital of France; Alsace-Lorraine—region in the northeast of France).
- list at least five attractions that the target country offers to the

tourist or the foreign student and design a poster or advertisement of the country for a travel agency.

For the city, the learner will:
- list three similarities and three differences between the city where the learner lives and that of the capital of the target country.
- list at least five places that the learner would visit in a specific city in the target country and describe the places.
- construct a postcard depicting one of the city's landmarks and write one comment about it.
- give at least three names of newspapers, magazines, products, cultural events, or activities that the learner thinks are different or interesting in the target country.
- name at least three customs that are different in the target country's society (e.g., traffic rules, etiquette, folklore, beliefs, holiday celebrations, etc.).

For shopping, the learner will:
- name at least five brand name products—items produced in, and/or exported by the target country.
- name at least two famous department stores, TV programs, or fashion shows, etc., from the target country.
- name at least three ways in which measuring systems are different in the target country (e.g., metric, different numbers for clothing or shoe sizes).
- recognize the target country's currency and determine its approximate value or equivalent in dollars.
- design a shopping list for buying a week's supply of food, gifts for family or friends, etc.

For food, the learner will:
- state at least three ways in which a menu in the target country is different from one in the U.S.
- list at least five to ten names of foods found in the target country which are commonly referred to in U.S. daily language.
- identify categories of five different dishes (e.g., dessert, main course, etc.) found in the target country.
- plan a dinner or design a menu indicating correct sequence of presentation, region of origin, and appropriate beverages.
- identify at least two different seasonings used in the target country.
- identify different meals of the day and the time when they are served.
- list three snack items commonly consumed in the target country and where they can be purchased.
- list two kinds of bread and their names found in the target country.
- name one beverage and one food item consumed or prepared during holidays or special occasions in the target country.
- name at least two different kinds of ice cream, candy, or pastry famous or popular in the target country.

Task Analysis

Baseline.   At least 90 percent of the class has had no formal exposure to the target language. Up to 10 percent may have studied the target language. We will assume that the students have no functional knowledge of the target language. They will have a grammatical awareness of their own native language; the extent of this awareness will be measured by the preassessment exam.

Target Unit.   Goal: Effective communication at a basic level in the target language.
Task analyzed objectives: The learner will:
* correctly form a sentence both orally and written in the target language.
* use correct written symbols.
* control sound system; pronounce correctly.
* use proper grammatical structure in writing and speaking.
* correctly answer a question, written or oral, or respond to a command or statement orally or in writing.

INSTRUCTIONAL PLAN

Scope of Unit

The focal points of our unit pertain to the grammar and culture of the target country.

Under the rubric *grammar,* we intend to promote the mastery of very basic language skills necessary for verbal communication. At the end of the unit, students will form four different types of sentences (declarative, interrogative, negative, and affirmative), correctly spell and pronounce designated words and sentences, and distinguish between a sentence which is syntactically and phonetically correct and one that is not. The students will know when and how to use the negative and how to conjugate the verb "to be" and regular first conjugation verbs. They will possess a vocabulary which will allow them to present ideas to others about themselves, others, and objects. They will correctly use gender markers, adjectives and forms of agreement and will read, write, and speak a very rudimentary form of the target language.

As the students study the grammar of the target language they will also observe patterns and rules, deductively apply these rules, and compare the target language to their own native language. The development of these skills, as well as the skills of analysis and synthesis, is the subpoint of our main focal point, grammar.

The following describes the purpose of the second focal point, culture. We want the students to approach and appreciate the target language via channels other than those of traditional language study. During the unit, we will cover four aspects of the culture of the target country. These lessons will continue throughout the year. The students will retain a basic impression of the similarities and the differences between the inhabitants of the target country and the members of their own culture. We intend to develop the skills of observation and promote the values of appreciation and tolerance of different cultures and subcultures. These skills and values will be measured by (1) student comments, (2) participation in class discussions, (3) increased positive interaction between students of different ethnic backgrounds, (4) heightened curiosity as testified by the students' questions and involvement.

A long-term objective that combines these two focal points will be a presentation by the students, given in the target language, on some aspect of the target country. The topic will be of the students' choice and will reflect some aspect of the culture of the target country that interests them. The successful completion of this project requires a mastery of the skills of communication and a minimal knowledge of the culture of the target country.

Major Activities

The following are generally included within each of the major activities:

Listening Comprehension. One of the key activities will be to train the students to listen and to try to locate words or familiar sentences in order to establish a meaning as the teacher presents new material. When the teacher or classmates dictate or spell for the learner, the learner must listen carefully to be able to distinguish the intonation and pronunciation patterns of the target language.

Speaking. Students will be using both English and the target language. During the culture sessions, students will be expected to participate and contribute opinions, ideas, questions, or suggestions in English. They will also present a brief oral report on their individual research project, making reference to notes.

Daily, when responding or correcting others in the target language, students will gradually increase their confidence with the language as their questions are better understood by the teacher and classmates. Occasionally, they will prepare questions or sentences to dictate to classmates. During games, they will demonstrate increasing mastery of the language.

Reading. Assigned reading will be given regularly to be done at home. The student will be responsible for all assigned readings as well as understanding passages at a descriptive level.

SCHEDULE OF ACTIVITIES

Week	Activity	Materials	Description
1 and 2	Presentation (in English) Oral activity Written activity Assignment	Tape recorder; maps of the world, Europe and target country; on day two, handout with information about the log.	Preassessment exam on native language ability. Introduction to the geographical location of the regions of the target country, its characteristics, major cities, and relevant geographical and historical landmarks. Tape with voices and noises. Demonstration on how to keep the log and hints on how to take notes for it and write observations. Assignment to locate and name on a blank map regions and landmarks shown in class, or to design a travel advertisement containing material covered in class. For next Friday's discussion assignment, students should bring a list of at least ten places that would be interesting to visit in a foreign city and turn it in on Thursday.
3	Correction Review Presentation (in English and target language) Oral activity Written activity Assignment	Paper and pencil Blackboard	Using the previous class material and assignment as anticipatory set, introduce a set of basic sentences which will be considered "idiomatic" because there will be no grammatical explanation about their components and/or structures. They will be used as references when students need to communicate their needs to the teacher (e.g., my name is _____; I don't understand; repeat please; how do you say _____?; how do you write _____?; etc.). At this point the list will be very short but it will be expanded as the course advances and the student's needs get more specific. Introduction to the concept of formal vs. familiar way to address a person using the idiomatic expression: ¿Cómo te llamas?/Comment t'appele-tu? ¿Cómo se llama Ud.?/Comment vous appelez-vous? Introduction to the alphabet. Vowels/vowel clusters in French; indicate that in Spanish, ch, ll, rr are one consonant and should be used as such when spelling; also emphasize those sounds that are different from English sounds.

SCHEDULE OF ACTIVITIES

Week	Activity	Materials	Description
			Assign exercise on formal *vs.* familiar, and formulate question using the idiomatic expression presented in class. Collect yesterday's assignment.
4	Correction Review Presentation in target language Oral activity Written activity Game and Quiz	Paper and pencil Blackboard; Cards for game (1 for each student with target language, names/surnames)	Review using correction of assignment on formal *vs.* familiar with classmates. Present *cómo/comment* as interrogative word that requests new information (in Spanish indicate that the accent is a feature of this type of word). Use the cards to have students go to the board while their classmates dictate the spelling of the names written on the cards and use this name when teacher or classmates ask, "What is your name?" Introduce the difference between *nombre/nom* and *apellido/nom-de-famille.* Assign to list five first names with five surnames that sound or look French/Spanish. Quiz.
5	Correction Review Presentation in target language	Paper and pencil Blackboard; Visual aids (depicting the times of day)	Correction of assignment. Review first name/surname, spelling, what is your name? Introduce greetings and at what time of day they are used. Introduce accepted abbreviations (e.g., SP: *Ud., Uds., Sr., Srta., Sra.;* F: *Mme, M, Mlle,* etc.). Only for Spanish: Introduce negative (e.g., *Yo no me llamo John Smith*). Assignment on greetings, use of abbreviations, and use of negative in Spanish.
6	Correction Review Presentation in target language	Paper and pencil Blackboard;	Correction of assignment. Review of greetings, abbreviations, and Spanish negative. Introduction of irregular verbs, *Ser/Etre,* with personal pronouns.

Oral activity Written activity	Visual aid (depicting 1 boy, 1 girl, 2 boys, and 2 girls)	Introduce interrogative word *quién/qui* (¿Quién es Ud.? Yo soy _____.) (Qui êtes-vous? Je suis _____.) Assignment.
7 Correction Review Presentation in target language Oral activity Written activity Game/quiz Assignment	Paper and pencil Blackboard Game cards (with country and city of origin) Visual aids	Correction/Quiz/Review "To be" and personal pronouns/interrogative word, *quién-qui*. Introduce numbers 1 to 10; Introduce interrogative word ¿De dónde es Ud.?/D'ou êtes-vous? -Yo soy de/Je suis de (country-city) Use cards to practice different countries and cities and visual aids to practice personal pronouns. Introduce yes/no vs. information type of questions and the adequate answer. (In French this difference has to be distinguished through intonation patterns, and the students will not be required to formulate the questions themselves.) Assignment.
8 Correction Review Presentation in target language Oral activity Written activity Game Assignment	Paper and pencil Blackboard; Game cards with nationality in masculine and feminine/ singular and plural	Correction/Review interrogatives/yes-no vs. infoquestions. Using the country/city of origin as an anticipatory set, introduce nationality without dwelling too much on the rules and/or their exceptions (use simple clear examples that do not present confusion or contradictions). In Spanish introduce interrogative word ¿qué es Ud.? Yo so (nationality). In French introduce the yes/no question Il/El/le est (nationality). Assignment on nationality, gender and number agreement.
9 Correction Review Presentation in target language Oral activity Written activity	Paper and pencil Blackboard; Game cards with telephone numbers; Handout for tomorrow's discussion	Correction/Review of nationality, numbers 1 to 10. Using numbers 1 to 10 as anticipatory set, introduce 10 to 30. Introduce interrogative word ¿cuál_____/quel_____? Incorporate telephone numbers; use the cards and ask students to answer using the numbers the way they are on the cards (individually or in pairs).

SCHEDULE OF ACTIVITIES

Week	Activity	Materials	Description
10	Quiz/game Assignment		Assignment: read handout for tomorrow's discussion on the city. Collect lists assigned last Monday.
	Review Presentation (in English) Oral activity (in both) Written activity (in English)	Paper and pencil Blackboard; Visual aids depicting city life and activities	Based on assignment given in previous culture session, and the handout given the day before, examine and talk about the city, its landmarks, parks, churches, museums, department stores, markets, monuments, rivers, transportation systems, newspapers-magazines, specialty stores, cinemas-movies, theaters, airports, etc. Assignment: chart a "tour" of the city with individual recommendations (expensive, reasonable, exotic, famous, elegant, etc.) or construct a postcard of the city with descriptive comments.
11	Collect assignment from culture session. Presentation of oral activity in target language Written activity in target language Game Assignment	Paper and pencil Blackboard; Cards with 2 addresses, 1 on each side, to use as own address and that of person to whom they are writing.	Review numbers 1 to 30/interrogative word *cuál/quel*. Introduce briefly possessive adj. for 1st and 2nd person singular. Introduce address and telephone number, and *nombre* and *apellido*/¿Cuál es su número de teléfono/nombre/apellido/ dirección? Quel est ton numéro de téléphone/nom/nom-de-famille?/Quelle est votre addresse? ¿Cuál es el número de teléfono de ellos/María? In Spanish, indicate the contraction de + el = del. Assignment: answer and formulate question applying these items.
12	Correction Review Presentation in target language Oral activity in target language	Paper and pencil Blackboard	Correction/Quiz/Review. Introduce days of the week and current month. Introduce difference between date and day and the adequate type of answer for each. In French, conclude presentation of prepositions: Quelle est la date aujourd'hui? Quel jour est-ce?

	Activities	Materials	Procedures
	Written activity in target language Quiz Assignment		Introduce vocabulary and indefinite article/interrogative ¿Qué es esto? Es una silla, un libro, etc. Assignment: answer and formulate questions using days-month-date-today-tomorrow
13	Correction Review Presentation Oral activity Written activity Game Assignment	Paper and pencil Blackboard; Game cards with professions on one side and descriptions on the other; Visual aids (depicting physical types)	Correction/Review. Using nationality as anticipatory set, introduce description (physical/mental) and professions with aid of game cards. Indicate use of different interrogative words (e.g., cómo—description; qué—profession. Incorporate review of preposition and definite article to indicate possession and apply to profession and description (e.g., ¿Cómo es el doctor de Jorge?). In French, introduce personal pronoun substitution and, briefly, affirmative vs. negative (e.g., C'est vs. ce n'est pas). Assignment.
14	Correction General review for midterm No presentation Oral activity Written activity No assignment	Paper and pencil Blackboard; Handout for midterm; Handout for tomorrow's discussion	Correction/Review. No assignment. Midterm on Monday. Bring questions on review handout. Questions reviewed/discussion on shopping. Examine ads and products advertised in target country (food, clothing, perfume, cars, beauty aids, housewares, etc).
15	Midterm Exam	Paper and pencil	Midterm Exam
16	Collect Friday's assignment on shopping Play tic-tac-toe Conduct interviews	Review the exam and the results Go over difficulties the majority of students had	Review the exam results and go over the difficulties that a majority of students had. Review vocabulary and play tic-tac-toe with "grammar devils". (In French, introduce the negative.) Assignment.
17	Correction Review	Paper and pencil Blackboard;	Correction/Review. Presentation of first conjugation regular verb hablar/parler.

SCHEDULE OF ACTIVITIES

Week	Activity	Materials	Description
	Presentation in target language Oral activity Written activity Assignment	Visual aid for 3rd person singular/plural and masculine/feminine; Visual aids for color; Cards for vocabulary review	Introduce colors and combine with possession (e.g., La pluma de María es roja). Introduce interrogative word: ¿De qué color es la pluma + de la doctora? ¿De quelle couleur est le stylo de Marie? Assignment.
18	Correction Review Presentation in target language Oral activity Written activity Assignment Handout material for tomorrow's discussion on food	Paper and pencil Blackboard; Visual aids for activity and/or sports, using regular verbs of the 1st conjugation. Handout for tomorrow's food discussion	Correction/Review of *hablar/parler* and its endings; personal pronouns. Use *preparar* and meals of the day. Introduce interrogative word: ¿Dónde+-AR verb+Relevant vocabulary (e.g., ¿Dónde nada Juan? Juan nada en la playa, el lago, etc. ¿Où nage Jean? Jean nage dans la mer, dans la piscine.) Quiz—*Hablar/parler.*
19	Correction Presentation Oral activity Written activity	Paper and pencil Blackboard; Visual aids Food types	Correction/Review. Food discussion based on handout given by teacher, and the assignment given last Friday to list food items that have a target language name, or target country's dishes or wines that sound familiar or have a target language origin.
20	Correction Review Presentation	Paper and pencil Blackboard; Clock;	Correction/Review. Introduce time and interrogative word ¿qué hora es? and ¿a qué hora + -AR verbs. Introduce time; indicate idiomatic way

Day	Activities	Materials	Content
	Oral activity Written activity Assignment	Visual aids on family	of expressing 1/2, 1/4, and 1/4 until; add seconds and minutes. In French, introduce singular *my* and *your* (*his* singular only). Introduce close family members (e.g., parents, brothers, and sisters) + possessive adjectives. Assignment.
21	Correction Review Presentation Oral activity Written activity Assignment	Paper and pencil Blackboard; Clock; Visual aids (parents-children-grandparents, husband, wife, uncle-aunt)	Correction/Review time-activities with -AR verbs and family members. Introduce grandparents-husband-wife, uncle-aunt in a family tree and add parents, children, brothers to it. In French only, introduce possessive adjectives "our" and "their" singular. In Spanish, introduce possessive adjectives. Assignment: design a family tree with description, profession, name, activity, place of origin, and time (Mi tío es doctor, él es hermano de mi papá. El es alto y gordo, él se llama Fred R. El es de México. Baila todos los sábados. Toma desayuna a las 8 A.M.)
22	Correction Review Presentation Oral activity Written activity Assignment	Paper and pencil Blackboard; Visual aids for seasons, months, and activities	Correction/Collect "Logs"/Review of total family. Introduce months of the year. Introduce seasons. Introduce birthday and interrogative word ¿cuándo . . ? Incorporate seasons, family members, and possessive adjectives in questions and sentences. Introduce weather expressions and apply to seasons. Assignment: go over review handout for final exam.
23	Correction Review No presentation Oral activity Written activity No assignment	Paper and pencil Blackboard; Review Handout	Correction/Review. No assignment.
24	FINAL EXAM	Paper and pencil	FINAL EXAM

In class sessions, on an individual basis, the student will need to be prepared to read aloud the assigned reading, dialogue, new material, or sentences written on the board. (S)he should be able to understand and spot errors. In a group, the student will participate in oral drills for pronunciation or substitution-type exercises.

Individual or group research will be conducted in English. The student will do a certain amount of reading to complete his/her individual research project on a certain country or subject related to the class.

Writing. Students will develop written communication skills when doing their homework or an assigned composition. During class, they will take notes, write on the board, and at certain times, take dictation. They will also write short assignments or exercises in class.

The students will take notes during the culture sessions and use them to create a log, in target language, along with generating compositions, dialogues, or cartoon strips containing original captions.

The six major in-class and out-of-class activities are:

Correction (10 to 15 minutes)
Review (10 minutes)
Presentation (20 minutes)
Assignment (5 minutes)
Discussion (1 hour each week)
Games (10 to 15 minutes)

Correction. This is done every day in the target language or in English in order to leave no room for misunderstanding.
- address mistakes found while correcting homework
- give immediate knowledge of results when correcting quiz in class
- reteach mistakes common to a number of students
- check for understanding of common mistakes
- mass practice in relation to common errors or for fast reinforcement of correct knowledge for those who were accurate

Review. This is done daily in the target language.
- provide for distributed practice
- motivate students, giving them confidence when they see that they are familiar with questions or words used during this period; provide questions students can answer easily and successfully
- check for understanding by going over or concentrating on problem points highlighted during correction
- provide anticipatory set for new material to be presented

Presentation. This is done daily in the target language.
- establish meaning by establishing relationship with previously studied material when presenting new concepts

- present content in brief, clear, and simple terms to avoid confusion or ambiguity
- use visual aids and effective modeling during this phase
- use guided practice with the group
- use mass practice for retention

Assignment.   This is assigned in the target language.
- establish a pleasant tone by offering choices when possible within assignments or by offering the alternative of writing the questions that the learner has regarding the homework instead of furnishing an answer
- motivate by showing the assignment is important and by collecting or dedicating time to it during correction
- use psychomotor activities; where appropriate point out relationships or parallels between the USA/English and the target country/target language

Discussion.   This is done weekly, in English.
- helps ease the tension and allows for much more material to be offered when conducted in English
- provides an organized and meaningful setting in the sense that students come prepared for the discussion with their own findings and ideas as well as being guided by a handout prepared by the teacher. This avoids wasting time trying to think of examples and ideas during class
- generates assignments which get students involved in designing their own projects, which stress originality, incorporate psychomotor skills, and establish relationships between their own culture and that of the target country
- promotes note taking and paying attention to what their classmates offer; they then incorporate this into their own logs

Games.   This is done in the target language.
- promotes the application of learned material to new situations
- provides variety in the classroom
- familiarizes the students with the untouchables of grammar; reinforces pronunciation, vocabulary, etc.
- provides for affective and psychomotor activities
- increases motivation when the students are competing for points

SECONDARY LESSON PLAN

Lesson Topic: _____ Negation: Review of Vocabulary _____

Unit Topic: _____ Spanish I _____ Grade Level: High School _____

1. INSTRUCTIONAL OBJECTIVE

The goal of the lesson is to present and practice the negation and review past vocabulary.

The objective will be implied, but not directly stated to the students. The objective will be specified for them at the end of the lesson.

The learner will:

- respond to review questions using appropriate grammar and vocabulary
- hear the introduction to the negation as modeled by the teacher (Q/A)
- respond to a question using the negation (with prompting from the teacher, if needed)
- write selected sentences on the board and in notes
- read and correct these sentences
- extract/state the rule for the negation with the guidance of the teacher
- copy the rule for the formation of the negation from the board into additional notes.
- correctly answer questions using the negation; practice use of the negative
- interview another student, asking questions that will elicit a negative response
- write the interview on a sheet of paper and turn it in
- respond to various questions asked by the teacher using correct grammar and vocabulary in order to win a tic-tac-toe space
- look at posters and pictures

    Homework: transform affirmative sentences into the negation; answer questions using the negation

2. MATERIALS

The students will write answers and sentences on the blackboard. *Objects* in the room, *pictures,* and *posters* will be used to initiate both affirmative and negative responses to specific questions.

3. MOTIVATION

Oral praise will be given: *bueno, perfecto, excelente.* Immediate knowledge of their performance will be given. Questions will be directed toward their interests, traits, and current events in a game format. The opportunity will be given to write their sentences on the board as a reward for the correct use of the negation. The teacher may also opt to initially stimulate interest in the topic by rhetorically asking the students, "How would you tell me that you aren't Spanish?"

Slow learners: Extra time and more prompts will be provided for these students. The responses of the other students will provide them with models. They will have the reinforcement of mass practice/response. They will be asked easier questions. During the interview session, slower students will be paired with advanced students who can help them ask and answer questions.

Advanced learners: The teacher will ask them more "difficult" questions. They may be asked to correct others. They will be asked to indicate the rule.

4. PROCEDURE

Anticipatory Set: "Buenos días!" Question-answer period reviewing past material covered.

Input Modalities: Oral, written, and visual. Discovery lesson. The teacher will present the concept in Spanish. The students will respond using the negative. The students will write on the board with the teacher's aid. They will read and correct these sentences and then deduce the rule.

Model: The teacher will orally demonstrate the concept and will write a sentence in the negation on the board if this is needed.

Checking/Evaluation: The teacher will check and evaluate comprehension during the presentation phase through question and answer, correcting mistakes, and using certain students as models (after they have demonstrated competency). The teacher may lengthen or shorten this period depending on student performance.

Guided-Practice: Done simultaneously with above. There will also be a period at the end of the lesson when the students will ask questions in pairs and correct themselves as the teacher circulates. It is also during this phase of the lesson that the teacher may evaluate how well the concept was learned and determine if any adjustments need to be made in the following plans or in the approaches used.

Activities: Review of exam and past concepts and vocabulary. Presentation of negative *orally* (question-answer) and *written* form (on board, in notes). *Games:* Interview between two students using the negative; a tic-tac-toe match game, with one side of the class competing against the other.

5. TIME ESTIMATES
Indicated on the script of the plan, next page.

6. EVALUATION
Did I vary the reinforcement? Was the pacing appropriate? When did the students seem most and/or least interested? Was there enough time for the students to benefit from the game? Did they feel lost? Should I have delayed the interview to the following day? Did the students act/look as though they were rushed or overloaded? Were any students upset when they were corrected by me or by other students? Were my transitions smooth?

7. INDEPENDENT WORK AND FOLLOW-UP
Homework exercises given. Correction of homework in class the following day. Review and practice of the negative during the following days.

SCRIPT TO ACCOMPANY LESSON

1. Buenos días, clase (2-5 minutes).

   ¿Cuál es la fecha de hoy?

   ¿Qué día es hoy?

   ¿Cuáles son los días de la semana?

   Cuenta de 1 a 20 (flash cards).

   Enseña una fotografía—¿cómo es X? ¿Es grande, pequeña, bonita, inteligente, etc.?

2. La Negación (20 minutes)

Teacher:	¿Qué es eso?
Student:	Un cuadro, un escritorio, un libro, un estudiante, una bolsa.
Teacher:	¿Dónde está X?
Teacher:	¿Cómo es X?
Teacher:	¿Somos inteligentes?
	americanos
	hispanos
Teacher:	No, no somos hispanos. Somos . . .
Teacher:	¿Estamos en la clase de biología?
Teacher:	No, no estamos . . . , estamos . . .
Teacher:	¿Estamos en la ciudad de México?
Teacher:	No, estamos en . . .
Teacher:	¿Están detrás de A y B (dos estudiantes)?
Teacher:	No, no están detrás de . . .
Teacher:	¿Soy hispano(a)?
Teacher:	No, no soy hispano(a) . . . .

   The preceding is the modeling done by the teacher. The students respond to the first series of questions that are in the affirmative.

Teacher:	¿Estamos en la clase de biología?
	¿Estamos en Chicago?
	¿Somos de la ciudad de México?
Student:	No, no estamos en la clase biología.

   (The sentences in typescript below are written on the board by the students.)

A	B
a. Estamos en la clase de español.	a. No estamos en la clase de biología.

Teacher:	Tú estás delante de X, detrás de X, entre Y y Z. Encima del escritorio, debajo de la mesa, en el suelo.

Student responds.

b. **Estoy sentado delante de X.**   b. **No estoy encima de la mesa.**

Fotos: ¿Quién es? (Señor y Señora Reagan)

Teacher: ¿Son hispanos? ¿Son de la ciudad de México?
¿Están en la Casa Blanca?
¿Son ricos, pobres?

Student responds.

c. **Sr. y Sra. Reagan están en la**   c. **No están en Los Angeles.**
Casa Blanca.

Teacher: ¿Eso es un _____?

Student: No, eso no es un _____; eso es un _____.

muchos objetos

Teacher: ¿Eso es el _____ de _____?

Student responds.

d. **Eso es el libro de Sarita.**   d. **Eso no es el lápiz de X.**

Fotos: ¿Quién es?

Teacher: Ella/él es rico(a), inteligente, bonito(a), grande.

Student responds.

Teacher: Ellos son . . .
Student responds.

e. _____ es _____.   e. **Sra. Dupont no es rica.**

Teacher: ¿Estoy delante de, detrás de, etc.?

Student responds.

f. **Tú estás delante de la clase.**   f. **Tú no eres hispana.**

Read and correct the sentences
Extract the rule:

Teacher: ¿Cuál es la diferencia entre A y B?
afirmativa y negativa   ¿cuántos partidos?
¿cuáles palabras?
¿la posición?

a la pizarra: *la negativa*
no + verb

3. Review and practice of the negation (5 minutes)

Teacher: ¿Tú estás parado(a)?
en la casa
en el edificio
estoy delante de/detrás de, etc.
los estudiantes son amables, están en la clase, están sentados,
son latinos.

4. Review and correction of the test (5–10 minutes)

5. Games

Interview: Ask questions of your partner that will elicit negative responses. Write down at least three of these answers. I will collect. (5–10 minutes)

Tic-Tac-Toe (remainder of time)

Divide class in half; ask questions regarding negative, past vocabulary, etc. Student must give a completely correct answer in order to choose a space.

6. Conclusion

Explain homework (at end of lesson plan); go over the model, "HASTA LUEGO"

HOMEWORK EXERCISES TO AUGMENT LESSON

1. Escriban en negativo:

   modelo: Soy de la ciudad de México.

   No soy de la ciudad de México.

   a. Eso es un libro.

   b. Eso es el escritorio de la señora.

   c. Soy Consuelo.

   d. María es grande.

   e. Pablo y Gregorio son americanos.

   f. Tú eres de los Estados Unidos.

   g. Estamos en Londres.

   h. La bolsa de ella está en el suelo.

   i. Estoy sentada adelante de Ricardo.

   j. Ellas son rubias.

   k. Juan y usted, ¿Ustedes son de la ciudad de México?

2. Conteste. Use la forma negativa.

   a. ¿Es usted hispano?

   b. ¿Está la profesora detrás del escritorio?

   c. ¿La clase de español es desde las ocho hasta las nueve?

   d. ¿Estamos en Chicago?

RESOURCES AND INSTRUCTIONAL MATERIALS

Student Materials and Texts to Be Used in the Unit

1. Text—*French I:*
   Valette and Valette, *French for Mastery.* Lexington, Mass.: D.C. Heath and Company, 1975.

2. Magazines:
   Paris Match, Salut les Copains, Michelin Guides.

3. Text—*Spanish I:*
   Valette, Jean-Paul, and Rebecca Valette, *Spanish for Mastery.* Lexington, Mass.: D.C. Heath and Company, 1980.

4. Other: notebook, writing instruments, blackboard.

Audiovisual Resources, Field Trips

1. Personal or departmental collection of slides, photos, post cards, posters, maps of target country, world map, map indicating where target language is spoken.

2. Tape recorder, projector, overhead projector.

3. French I: film series—*En Francais,* Didier Publications

Additional Material or Ideas

1. Games: concentration (form proper sentence); menu game; bingo; cross-word puzzles; cartoon strips without headings which student must complete; games without any tools except chalkboard and/or poster.

2. Visitors: friends; local merchants; consulate members as guest speakers.

3. Songs: to be sung when time allows or when the students are bored; special songs for holidays

Bibliography

1. Books:
   Blunt, Anthony, Sir. *French Art and Music Since 1500.* London: Methuen, New York: Harper and Row, 1974.
   Brichant, Colette Dubois. *La France au Cours des Ages.* New York: McGraw-Hill, 1973.
   Darbelnet, J.L. *Pensee et Structure.* New York: Charles Scribner's Sons, 1969.
   Grevisse, Maurice. *Precis de Grammaire Francaise.* Paris-Gembloux: Editions Duculot, 1969.
   Linder, Cathey, ed. *Oral Communication Testing. Skokie,* Illinois: National Textbook Company, 1977.

Service Pedagogique-Ambassade de France. *Parlons Francais.*
Mexico City, n.d.

Stroller, Phyllis-Hersh, Joanne Lock, Virginia Wilson, and
Beverly Wattenmaker. *Real Communication in French.* Upper
Jay, New York: The Adirondack Mountain Humanistic Ed-
ucation Center, n.d.

2. Periodicals:

Foreign Language Annals. Hastings-on-Hudson. New York:
ACTFL.

French Review. Champaign, Illinois: American Association of
Teachers of French.

Gourmet. Boulder, Colorado: Gourmet, Inc.

EVALUATION PROCEDURES

This section contains the essential steps taken in evaluating students before,
during, and after instruction. Sample instruments are provided where appropriate.

Preassessment

Prior to implementing the unit, we will administer a test to determine the
minimal reading and writing levels of the students. The test will be designed
to assess to what extent the students are aware of the grammatical components of their native language, assuming that this is English. If this is not the
case, the native language should be taken into consideration in two ways:
one as the disadvantage it would present for vocabulary or culture sections
done in English; the other as an asset since the student has already learned
the process of second language acquisition. Once the percentages have been
established as to how many know what content, the approach criteria can be
adjusted accordingly.

If very few students know grammatical components, the teacher should introduce the name and functions of verbs, nouns, and adjectives. The teacher
should also apply these terms and functions every time there is an opportunity to
do so. Hopefully, the students will lose their fear of the terms and will be more
comfortable using them once they are able to identify them and apply them to
other situations.

Formative Evaluation

There will be several levels at which the students will be evaluated. First, they
will be assessed daily as the teacher evaluates and corrects errors in structure,

PREASSESSMENT FORM

If you were an alien, recently arrived in Los Angeles, what would you find the most interesting? Why? What would you do first, and what would you try to learn first? Why? (You have fifteen minutes. Please use complete sentences.)

_____

_____

_____

_____

_____

Diagram the following sentences: (You have ten minutes.)

Harry is not handsome; he is ugly.

The boy, who is talking to my mother, speaks four languages.

I am looking for a book.

ASSESSING THE STRATEGIC PLANNING OF A TEACHING UNIT

Unit Topic: __First Five Weeks of French I/Spanish I__   Grade Level: __High School__

1. BACKGROUND INFORMATION
    a. Is the background information provided adequate in conveying the underlying philosophy of the unit? Yes __X__ No _____
    b. Does the background information provide a concise profile of the learners?
       Yes __X__ No _____

Comments: The lesson contains a clear description of its underlying philosophy

and a clear profile of the learners. Perhaps some statements regarding a

philosophy of language teaching/learning would be appropriate here also.

2. UNIT DESCRIPTION
    a. Does the unit description offer a clear explanation of the rationale for implementing the unit? Yes __X__ No _____
    b. Are the goals and objectives of the unit:
       • Clearly stated? Yes __X__ No _____
       • Comprehensive enough to support the planned scope of the unit?
         Yes __X__ No _____ (very comprehensive)

Comments: Given the underlying rationale espoused for this unit, it is both in-

novative and engaging. The objectives are clearly stated in observable terms,

and the categories are helpful in conceptualizing the scope of the unit. How-

ever, many of the objectives are applied only to the teaching of Spanish and

do not include the equivalent application to teaching French. (See objectives 1,

4, 10, and 11 under Grammar category.)

3. INSTRUCTIONAL PLAN
    Task Analysis. Is the task analysis complete in terms of providing:
    • A clear and sound assessment of entry-level behavior?
      Yes __X__ No _____ (*See below)
    • Appropriate and comprehensive intermediate steps?
      Yes __X__ No _____ (**See below)
    • A complete set of target behaviors which match the instructional objectives?
      Yes _____ No __X__ (Partially ***See below)

b. Activities. Are the scheduled activities:
  • Sufficiently comprehensive to achieve the planned objectives?
    Yes __X__ No _____
  • Presented in a logical sequence so as to maximize the achievement of the objective? Yes __X__ No _____
  • Clearly stated with sufficient amplification to provide a clear instructional picture of their intent? Yes __X__ No _____

c. Sample Daily Lesson Plans. Does the sample daily lesson plan:
  • Model a sound and comprehensive lesson plan? Yes __X__ No _____
  • Lead to the mastery of the stated objectives? Yes __X__ No _____

Comments: The activities are well conceptualized by categories; they are comprehensive throughout the unit plan and build on previous knowledge and success. The activities chosen show much thought and creativity. We would suggest that the actual games be more clearly described. The lesson plan is well-presented and challenging. It may take on "too much" content. The concept of negation appears especially well-presented.

*Adequate, could be improved through expanding; is too general.
**Concise yet sound.
***Not done in this form exactly; general steps, however, match the categories.

4. RESOURCES AND INSTRUCTIONAL MATERIALS
    Are the resources and instructional materials used in the unit:
      • Comprehensive enough to support the unit? Yes __X__ No _____
      • Oriented toward a variety of learning styles? Yes __X__ No _____

Comments: A variety of learning styles were accommodated in the unit design. Additionally, there was effective use of auditory reinforcement materials, visual aids, and board work.

5. EVALUATION PROCEDURES
    a. Preassessment. Is the preassessment planned for the unit:
      • Appropriate for the learners? Yes __X__ No _____ (*See below)
      • Adequate for the planned objectives?
        Yes _____ No __X__ (Partially, **See below)
    b. Formative Evaluation. Are the criterion checks adequate enough to ensure ongoing mastery of the unit objectives?
      Yes __X__ No _____ (Could be more fully explained in terms of the scheduling; perhaps a chart or record sheet could be provided.)

c. Unit Evaluation. Does the unit evaluation:
  • Include all target instructional objectives?
    Yes __X__ No _____ (final exam provides this)
  • Provide for adequate teacher and student input?
    Yes _____ No _____ (Partially)

Comments: It could be a more useful unit evaluation if student questionnaires were given in addition to the exam to determine the effectiveness of the approach used in the unit. Were attitudes changed, etc.? Also, the preassessment calls for students to diagram sentences. How many students know how to do this in English?

*Reading and writing assessed.
**May want to include foreign language assessment to determine previous knowledge.

pronunciation, etc., on the spot. Also daily there will be homework by which the teacher can determine what points in the previous lesson presented the most difficulties to the students. Next, there will be formal quizzes given daily or biweekly. The quizzes will include the previously studied material and can be used, once corrected, as a reference for more comprehensive examinations. Weekly, there will be a written assignment in English so that the teacher may assess the students' comprehension and appreciation of the cultural sections of the unit. Finally, there will be two exams; one is to be administered at midpoint and the other at the end of the five weeks.

Unit Evaluation

At the conclusion, the entire unit will be evaluated based upon degree of importance of one aspect in relation to the rest of the unit. The criteria used will be as follows: the average total of all the quizzes will count as twenty percent of the final grade. The average total of all homework will count as twenty percent. There will be a twenty percent value given for the oral participation and a forty percent value for the average of the two more comprehensive exams.

This evaluation is intended to be as fair and beneficial to the students as possible. Our unit evaluation does not strongly penalize for weaknesses or negligence in one aspect despite the accomplishment in the rest. It also takes into consideration factors such as personality differences (shyness, etc.) that may prevent students from excelling in certain domains.

FURTHER READINGS

Brown, James W., Richard Lewis, and Fred Harcleroad. *AV Instruction: Technology, Media, and Methods.* New York: McGraw-Hill, Inc., 1983.

Gronlund, Norman. *Stating Objectives for Classroom Instruction,* 3rd ed. New York: Macmillan Co., 1985.

Hunter, Beverly. *My Students Use Computers: Learning Activities for Computer Literacy.* Alexandria, Va.: Human Resources Research Organization, 1983.

Johnston, Hiram, Shirley Haley-James, Buckly Barnes, and Ted Colton. *The Learning Center Idea Book.* Boston: Allyn and Bacon, 1978.

Popham, James W. *Criterion-Referenced Measurement.* Englewood Cliffs, N.J.: Prentice-Hall, Inc., 1978.

Popham, James W. *The Uses of Instructional Objectives.* Belmont, Calif.: Fearon Publishing, 1973.

Sharan, Shlomo, and Yael Sharan. *Small-Group Teaching.* Englewood Cliffs, N.J.: Education Technology, 1976.

Sleeman, Phillip, Ted Cobun, and D. W. Rockwell. *Instructional Media and Technology.* New York: Longman, 1979.

Tashne, John H., ed. *Improving Instruction with Microcomputers: Readings and Resources for Elementary and Secondary Schools.* Phoenix, Ariz.: Oryx Press, 1984.

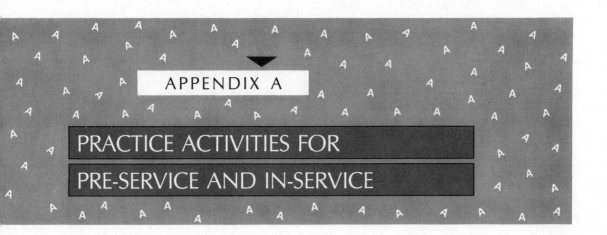

APPENDIX A

PRACTICE ACTIVITIES FOR
PRE-SERVICE AND IN-SERVICE

Curriculum Development Activities
Chapter One

1. Select a grade level and subject area (e.g., seventh-grade English), and write three complete instructional objectives that would be appropriate for students in this class. (See pp. 2–10.)

2. Using the "Albatross" example on p. 6, select a topic and grade level, and create a set of questions and/or activities that correspond to the six levels of Bloom's Taxonomy.

3. Select a grade level, and list three activities that would promote the affective development of these students. Correlate the activities with the five levels of the affective domain. (See pp. 7–8.)

4. Select a grade level and a skill area (e.g., tenth grade, commas). Explain one approach you might take in preassessing learners relative to this skill. Justify your selection. (See pp. 10–11.)

5. Select a grade level and a skill area (e.g., third grade, compound words). Create a task analysis for an appropriate instructional sequence to promote this skill. (See pp. 12–14.)

Learning and Instruction Activities
Chapter Two

6. Observe a classroom for at least one hour, of which at least twenty minutes are devoted to instruction. Using the list of eight learning principles discussed in Chapter Two, analyze the instruction in terms of effective or ineffective use of these principles. When appropriate, provide suggestions for a more effective application of the given principles. (See pp. 15–27.)

7. Using the guidelines provided in Chapter Two, write a complete lesson plan for a designated grade level. (See pp. 27–30.)

8. Select one of the three models of classroom discipline discussed in Chapter Two, and explain the basic strengths and weaknesses of the model. Include why you would or would not choose to apply this model in your classroom. If possible, try to find a classroom in which this model is being implemented, and observe the model in action for the purpose of this analysis. (See pp. 30–34.)

9. Observe a lecture presented to a class by an instructor. Analyze its relative success or failure using the criteria for effective communication presented in Chapter Two. Discuss specific ways in which the communicative process could have been improved. Analyze the role communication played (negative or positive) relative to the proposed instructional intent of the sequence. (See pp. 34–39.)

Evaluation Activities
Chapter Three

10. Select a grade level; find subject area content appropriate to the grade level (e.g., eighth grade, famous U.S. inventors in the nineteenth century). Textbooks and encyclopedias are good sources. Using the specifications for effective teacher-made test construction outlined in Chapter Three, create a twenty-item test appropriate for the learners based on the specific content. (See pp. 44 –46.)

11. Interview two to four students on the topic of grades. Using these ideas, respond in writing (e.g., poem, essay) to the issue of grading students. (See pp. 46–48.)

Modular Learning Center Activity
Chapter Four

12. Select a grade level and subject area or skill. Then select one of the three types of modular learning centers discussed in Chapter Four that could address these students. Design, on paper, a learning center containing the essential elements on the learning center checklist (p. 58). Include a written rationale for the center and description of its intended use.

Experience-Based Instruction Activity
Chapter Five

13. Select a grade level; write a role-playing dilemma that relates to these students. If possible, have volunteers enact the role-playing; you lead the follow-up debriefing session. (See example p. 66.)

Inquiry-Based Instruction Activity
Chapter Six

14. Select a grade level and subject area. Select either discovery-oriented or policy-based inquiry. Generate a list of three to five inquiry topics that would be appropriate and engaging for these learners. Provide a brief justification of your selection (i.e., why these would be appropriate; why you consider these to be *inquiry* topics).

Student-Centered Advocacy Learning Activity
Chapter Seven

15. Select a grade level. Generate a list of three to five debate topics that would be appropriate for these learners. Justify your selection in terms of the essential characteristics of a topic that must be included. (See pp. 82–84.)

Instructional Strategies Activity
Chapters Four–Seven

16. Select one of the instructional approaches discussed in Chapters Four, Five, Six, or Seven. Summarize its essential characteristics, explain the rationale for its use, and analyze it in terms of its potential value for your students.

Technology-in-the-Classroom Activity
Chapter Eight

17. Select a grade level and subject area. Find a piece of audiovisual or computer-based curriculum, and analyze its effectiveness for these learners. If possible, try to use the resource with students before evaluating its effectiveness.

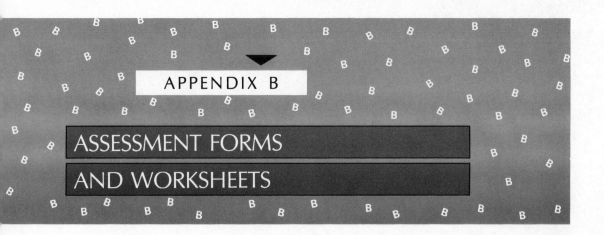

APPENDIX B

ASSESSMENT FORMS

AND WORKSHEETS

SOFTWARE PROGRAM EVALUATION

Program Name: _____

Subject Area: _____ Grade Level: _____

1. INSTRUCTIONAL OBJECTIVES OF PROGRAM

_____

_____

_____

_____

_____

_____

INSTRUCTIONAL NEEDS OF STUDENTS ADDRESSED BY PROGRAM

_____

_____

_____

_____

_____

_____

CONDITIONS FOR USE

_____

_____

_____

_____

_____

_____

2. TO EVALUATE THIS PROGRAM, A TEAM COULD:

_____

_____

_____

_____

_____

3. QUALITY OF THE PROGRAM

_____

_____

_____

_____

_____

_____

4. INTERACTIVE QUALITY OF PROGRAM

_____

_____

_____

_____

_____

_____

5. TEACHER TIME AND ASSISTANCE REQUIRED

_____

_____

_____

_____

_____

_____

6. OTHER COMMENTS

_____

_____

_____

_____

_____

ASSESSING THE STRATEGIC PLANNING OF THE LESSON PLAN

Lesson Topic: _____ Grade Level: _____

1. INSTRUCTIONAL OBJECTIVES

    a. Are the objectives stated operationally and in precise and measurable terms?
    Yes _____ No _____

    b. Are the objectives developmentally well chosen? Yes _____ No _____

Comments: _____

_____

_____

2. MATERIALS

    a. Are the instructional materials appropriate for meeting the objectives?
    Yes _____ No _____

    b. Are the instructional materials adequate to provide accommodation to different
    learning styles? Yes _____ No _____

Comments: _____

_____

_____

3. MOTIVATION

    a. Are the motivational techniques incorporated into the lesson adequate for
    generating an interest in the lesson? Yes _____ No _____

    b. Are the motivational techniques incorporated into the lesson adequate in terms of
    maintaining and sustaining an interest in the lesson?
    Yes _____ No _____

Comments: _____

_____

_____

4. PROCEDURE

    a. Are the teacher and learner roles/activities during the lesson clearly outlined and
    explained? Yes _____ No _____

    b. Are the activities in the instructional sequence congruent with the lesson's
    objectives? Yes _____ No _____

    c. Is the lesson plan logically sequenced? Yes _____ No _____

d. Do the activities in the lesson provide for individual differences in learning? Yes _____ No _____

e. Do the activities in the lesson represent clear examples of the effective use of learning principles? Yes _____ No _____

Comments: _____

_____

_____

5. TIME ESTIMATES

a. Are the time estimates in the lesson appropriately paced? Yes _____ No _____

b. Are the time estimates in the lesson realistic? Yes _____ No _____

Comments: _____

_____

_____

6. EVALUATION

a. Is the evaluation of the lesson appropriate in terms of assessment of completed objectives? Yes _____ No _____

b. Is the evaluation of the lesson appropriate in terms of assessment of the overall success of the lesson design? Yes _____ No _____

Comments: _____

_____

_____

7. INDEPENDENT WORK AND FOLLOW-UP

a. If independent work is assigned, does such work provide appropriate practice to reinforce the stated objectives? Yes _____ No _____ Not applicable _____

b. If follow-up assignments are included, do they enhance the stated goals of the lesson plan? Yes _____ No _____ Not applicable _____

Comments: _____

_____

_____

_____

ASSESSING THE STRATEGIC PLANNING OF THE TEACHING UNIT

Lesson Topic: _____ Grade Level: _____

1. BACKGROUND INFORMATION

   a. Is the background information provided adequate for conveying the underlying philosophy of the unit?   Yes _____   No _____

   b. Does the background information provide a concise profile of the learners? Yes _____   No _____

Comments: _____

_____

_____

_____

2. UNIT DESCRIPTION

   a. Does the unit description offer a clear explanation of the rationale for implementing the unit?   Yes _____   No _____

   b. Are the goals and objectives of the unit:

      • Clearly stated?   Yes _____   No _____

      • Comprehensive enough to support the planned scope of the unit? Yes _____   No _____

Comments: _____

_____

_____

_____

3. INSTRUCTIONAL PLAN

   a. Task Analysis. Is the task analysis complete in terms of providing:

      • A clear and sound assessment of entry-level behavior? Yes _____   No _____

      • Appropriate and comprehensive intermediate steps? Yes _____   No _____

      • A complete set of target behaviors which match the instructional objectives?   Yes _____   No _____

   b. Activities. Are the scheduled activities:

      • Sufficiently comprehensive to achieve the planned objectives? Yes _____   No _____

- Presented in a logical sequence so as to maximize the achievement of the objective? Yes _____   No _____
- Clearly stated with sufficient amplification to provide a clear instructional picture of their intent? Yes _____   No _____

c. Sample Daily Lesson Plans. Does the sample daily lesson plan:
  - Model a sound and comprehensive lesson plan? Yes _____   No _____
  - Lead to the mastery of the stated objectives? Yes _____   No _____

Comments: _____

_____

_____

_____

4. RESOURCES AND INSTRUCTIONAL MATERIALS

Are the resources and instructional materials used in the unit:
- Comprehensive enough to support the unit? Yes _____   No _____
- Oriented toward a variety of learning styles? Yes _____   No _____

Comments: _____

_____

_____

_____

5. EVALUATION PROCEDURES

a. Preassessment. Is the preassessment planned for the unit:
  - Appropriate for the learners? Yes _____   No _____
  - Adequate for the planned objectives? Yes _____   No _____

b. Formative Evaluation. Are the criterion checks adequate to ensure on-going successful mastery of the unit objectives? Yes _____   No _____

c. Unit Evaluation. Does the unit evaluation:
  - Include all target instructional objectives? Yes _____   No _____
  - Provide for adequate teacher and student input?
    Yes _____No _____

Comments: _____

_____

_____

ASSESSING THE QUALITY OF COMMUNICATION IN THE INSTRUCTIONAL SEQUENCE

1 = needs a great deal of work
2 = needs some work
3 = competent
4 = excels

1. Ethos of Sender (Poise, Security)

    1   2   3   4

Comments: _____

_____

_____

2. Ethos of Sender (Psychological Dominance)

    1   2   3   4

Comments: _____

_____

_____

3. Delivery: Voice

    1   2   3   4

Comments: _____

_____

_____

4. Delivery: Mannerisms

    1   2   3   4

Comments: _____

_____

_____

5. Digressions (Comfortable/Uncomfortable)

1   2   3   4

Comments: _____

_____

_____

6. Clarity of Message (Explaining Content and Giving Directions)

1   2   3   4

Comments: _____

_____

_____

7. Use of Concrete Examples

1   2   3   4

Comments: _____

_____

_____

8. Effective Use of Repetition

1   2   3   4

Comments: _____

_____

_____

9. Effective Use of Summarization (Formative/Summative)

1   2   3   4

Comments: _____

_____

_____

FOLLOW THE LEAD!

Label the facts in numbers 1 and 2 below *Who, What, When, Where, Why,* and *How.* The problems may *not* contain an example of all six possible question words. After you have labeled them, write a news lead using the facts. Remember—be informative *and* exciting! For number 3, write your own set of facts and an original news lead using them.

1. a. He was invited by the school to discuss crime
   b. A policeman
   c. Yesterday
   d. In the auditorium
   e. To talk to sixth-graders

2. a. Last week
   b. Voted
   c. 100 sixth-graders
   d. In the cafeteria
   e. In order to support the candidates

3. Write your own news lead. Write down your facts first, label them, and then write your lead. This is your chance to *lead* your way to becoming a famous journalist. Good luck!

_____

_____

_____

_____

_____

_____

_____

From *Effective Teaching,* by Marilyn Kourilsky and Lory Quaranta, Copyright © 1987 Scott, Foresman and Company.

KNOW YOUR NEWSPAPER!

A newspaper is a tremendous source all types of news, ideas, and interesting information. Your assignment is to get acquainted with newspapers by discovering the different features a newspaper contains.

Below is a list of new topics. You are to find an article on *each* topic. Glue, tape, or staple each clipping neatly onto a piece of paper, labeling each page. Make your own notebook or purchase one; it's up to you. Your newspaper notebook is something to be proud of!

1. World news
2. National news
3. State news
4. Local news
5. Editorials (opinions)
6. Sports
7. Weather
8. Comics (comic strips)
9. Political cartoon
10. Classified ads
11. Financial news—the stock market
12. Movie reviews
13. Letters-to-the-editor
14. "Dear Abby" letter
15. Anything else you would like to add

Have fun getting to know your newspaper! You'll be glad you did!

GET THE FACTS!

Write down *five* important facts from this story. Many facts are important, but you may only choose FIVE!

"Friends of Carthay," a parent volunteer group, put on a Halloween Breakfast October 30, 1983, on the playground, in order to raise money for the school.

Pancakes, sausage, and orange juice were served by the parents. In addition to the food sale, there was a haunted house and a sweatshirt booth where everyone could buy sweatshirts.

Many children dressed up in their Halloween costumes, and it seemed like fun was had by all.

Fact 1 _____

Fact 2 _____

Fact 3 _____

Fact 4 _____

Fact 5 _____

FAMOUS JOURNALISTS

For Group Work and Learning Center

1. John Peter Zenger—*New York Weekly Journal* 1733 "Free Press"
2. Benjamin Harris—First American newspaper
3. Benjamin H. Day—Penny newspaper
4. Horace Greeley—*New York Tribune*
5. William Randolph Hearst—Sensationalism
6. Joseph Pulitzer—Sensationalism
7. Edward Wyllis Scripps—First chain newspaper
8. Benjamin Franklin
9. Walter Lippman
10. William F. Buckley, Jr.

This is a teacher's aid. Names of the six most interesting and easily researched journalists will be assigned to group work, while the other journalists will appear in the learning center.

PREASSESSMENT FORM

If you were an alien, recently arrived in Los Angeles, what would you find the most interesting? Why? What would you do first, and what would you try to learn first? Why? (You have fifteen minutes. Please use complete sentences.)

_____

_____

_____

_____

_____

Diagram the following sentences: (You have ten minutes.)

Harry is not handsome; he is ugly.

The boy, who is talking to my mother, speaks four languages.

I am looking for a book.

From *Effective Teaching*, by Marilyn Kourilsky and Lory Quaranta, Copyright © 1987 Scott, Foresman and Company.

INDEX

Also Available from
Scott, Foresman and Company
Good Year Books

Good Year Books are reproducible resource and activity books for teachers and parents of students in preschool through grade 12. Written by experienced educators, Good Year Books are filled with class-tested ideas, teaching strategies and methods, and fun-to-do activities for every basic curriculum area. They also contain enrichment materials and activities that help extend a child's learning experiences beyond the classroom.

Good Year Books address many educational needs in both formal and informal settings. They have been used widely in preservice teacher training courses, as a resource for practicing teachers to enhance their own professional growth, and by interested adults as a source of sound, valuable activities for home, summer camp, Scout meetings, and the like.

Good Year Books are available through your local college or university bookstore, independent or chain booksellers, and school supply and educational dealers. For a complete catalog of Good Year Books, write:

Good Year Books
Department PPG-T
1900 East Lake Avenue
Glenview, Illinois 60025